SHENANIGANS

SHENANIGANS

A MEMOIR

Abby Kenigsberg

SHENANIGANS
A MEMOIR

iUniverse books may be ordered through booksellers or by contacting:

iUniverse
1663 Liberty Drive
Bloomington, IN 47403
www.iuniverse.com
1-800-Authors (1-800-288-4677)

ISBN: 978-1-5320-9751-5 (sc)
ISBN: 978-1-5320-9757-7 (e)

Print information available on the last page.

iUniverse rev. date: 03/17/2020

This Book Is Dedicated to

My Three Sons
with Love and Laughter

CONTENTS

PART FOUR
COUPLING 201

PART FIVE
FLYING

PART SIX
MOVING UP

PART SEVEN
SOMEONE TO WATCH OVER ME

PART EIGHT
GOODBYE

FOREWORD

EDITORS ARE NO FUN

I was supposed to be called "Gertrude." That was the plan. In memory of Daddy's grandma. But Mother thought "Gertrude" didn't have much charm.

"Abigail," she thought, was more beguiling, and that the *g* in the third syllable would honor Gertrude's memory just fine. Then, at the last minute, someone thought "Abby" had even more charm—and that was that.

Best I can remember, no one actually *told* me to be charming, wear nice clothes, and marry a doctor. But I did all three. I married the doctor and concentrated on his needs, my charm, and our clothes.

When my first son was born, I was surprised to learn that I desperately wanted to get out of the house from time to time. I worked in radio, then cable, then became the founding executive director of the Long Island Coalition for Fair Broadcasting, Inc., on Long Island, New York (1979–2001).

The organization's purpose was to press New York City-based TV stations to provide more responsible news coverage for suburban Long Island. It bugged me that the TV stations that had an obligation to serve suburban Long Island were reaping profits from our rich market while ignoring their public service obligations.

I loved the job and worked hard for its success. While I worked, I wrote what I thought were funny chapters about how clueless I was, the plots I devised for better coverage, and the worthwhile fundraisers we developed. I had a scoop on some of the people I met, including Dan Rather, Leslie Stahl, Alan King, and Mike Wallace.

Yet after seventeen years, the zest of creating a new organization had faded. The major goals had been achieved to some extent. We'd started a revolution in Long Island news coverage. The Coalition had generated enthusiasm about our home community, the TV stations had contributed some fine Long Island news stories, and community leaders had acquired some expertise in explaining their work to TV stations. I wanted a new challenge. It was painful to give up the job, but I did. I put the chapters about the Coalition years in the back of a file cabinet and focused on the future.

A few years later my son Matthew convinced my husband and me to move to a city where one of our three sons could keep track of us as we grew older. Just as Ken and I were about to leave for Austin, Texas, I grabbed the almost forgotten Coalition memoir from the file cabinet.

Once we had resettled, I asked an editor in Austin if I had a good story.

"Oh, Abby," she said, "people don't care about someone's success. They want to hear about what *didn't* work on the job. About how you juggled marriage and work. About the personal challenges that smacked you in the face."

I asked my son Ezra if the editor was right.

"Yeah," he replied, "she's right. I just finished reading Madeleine Albright's autobiography, *Madam Secretary.* She talks about how tough it was to get divorced. Someone came up to her and said, 'You have it all.' And Madeleine said, 'I didn't have it all. I was full of self-pity. I was always thinking about what I lost, not what I had.'"

Damn, I thought. *Do I have to confess the problems of living with a guy who, like me, always wanted to be the Big Cheese?* He was the most interesting man I ever met. But he had no idea how to take turns in a conversation. It was always his turn.

Do I have to talk about my mom, an especially talented pianist and romantic, who racked up some pretty nadir moments for herself and for me?

And do I have to admit my own negatives? Like when I locked my sleeping infant in the back of the car in a parking lot in sleepy Huntington, Long Island, just for a job interview?

I decided this would be tough, so I stuffed the writing back in the file cabinet. I kept the glossy picture of Dan Rather and me for old times' sake. But I kept thinking about this seemingly impossible task. I realized I wanted to write the story because it *was* impossible.

Here it is.

PART ONE

EARLY DAYS

SHAVING

The clapboard farmhouse at 94 Alpine Avenue in Bridgeport, Connecticut (where I grew up), was narrow—skinny even. The outside was a whitish-grey color. Inside was no different. The bathroom on the second floor had worn-out linoleum and white walls. Yet it managed to stay dark since no sunlight could reach it. The sink was a single pedestal covered in a grey, tired enamel. Reflecting all the grey from every angle was the boxy mirrored cabinet above it, a square bump on a wall.

But I liked the bathroom. It was where Daddy shaved every morning and I could get into the action. He would stand there with his sleepy, wrinkled skin and fuzzy hair, holding his razor carefully to remove his nightly growth with ritual-like motions, letting me watch. Me, by the side of the sink, standing ever so still, my nose level with the string of his pajamas. With his gentle smile and his exact motions, everything about that man made me feel safe.

First he would get the straight razor from the medicine chest and snap it open. The razor, newly exposed, would gleam. It was the only gleaming thing in the grey light.

"Why does the sun shine in the morning and not at night, Daddy?" He would be at the far end of the bathroom holding the leather strop taut and sliding the razor up and down to sharpen it. Then he would return the strop to its special hook.

Now he would be back at the sink and he'd open the cabinet door and take his shaving mug from its place on the shelf.

"Huh, Daddy? Huh, Daddy?"

He would pass the mug under the faucet he'd turned on with a quarter turn. He would add just enough water to the mug to get the dry shaving soap lathered up, using the soft brush that always sat in the mug. He would smile at me. "The Earth goes around the sun, honeybunch. We're away from the sun at night, and by the morning we have a chance to see it again."

By now he would have painted the puffy soap all over his cheeks and chin, carefully around his mustache, looking steadily in the mirror.

"How come the driveway's so long, Daddy?" He would put a tiny drop of the fluffy soap on my nose. "No, really, Daddy. How come it's so long, Daddy? Huh, Daddy? How come?"

He would put the mug back in its place on the shelf and bring up his hand to begin to shave. Then he would put the blade down, smiling. "Because Mr. Griffin built the garage way in the back so you and your sister would have a yard to play in, honeybunch."

He would lift the razor again and put it on the side of his face with great care. He would quickly glide it down his cheek. It would make a gritty noise. Then he would shave the other side in exact symmetry. Next he would raise his chin high and shave the underside from left to right with sure strokes. He would snap the suds off the razor into the sink, put his chin down, curl his upper lip around his teeth, and, getting still closer to the mirror, trim around his mustache with short strokes.

"Daddy, where's the sun when it's cloudy? Huh, Daddy? Where's the sun when it's cloudy?"

He'd stop trimming. "It's there, honeybunch. It's high up and above the thick clouds."

He would finish the mustache trim, having checked for recalcitrant hairs. Satisfied with the outcome, he would wipe the razor on a towel, close it, and return it to its place in the cabinet.

Then he would take the Old Spice bottle, open it, and put the stopper in the same spot he did yesterday, pour just two drops into each palm, and gently clap his hands together and slap his cheeks. I would stand up straight by his side to receive my portion, and he would gently tap my cheeks with what was left. I loved the fresh smell. And I felt important with the application.

"Have a good day in school, honeybunch," he would always say as we left the grey bathroom together.

CHINESE WALLPAPER

I was maybe four. Rebellion and mischief took up significant parts of my day.

I didn't like the major disciplinary event that was unfolding. Mother was incensed because for a couple of months I'd been writing on the walls of the house.

Eavesdropping behind a door one day, I overheard Daddy tell guests that in order to get me to stop writing on the wall, he'd bought a huge pad of paper and hung it in the living room. He chuckled as he told them that as a result of his plan, I'd put two marks on the paper and then one mark on the wall.

The contest of wills was at a standstill. There were marks on the wall and commands for obedience, and on the day in question Mother was leaving for a very important party. She was wearing the dress that turned from lavender to blue when it swished. She talked about the dress a lot. It had a round neck and a big skirt, and that's the dress I voted for her to wear at my birthday party. She let me touch it if I washed my hands. Anyway, that was the day I drew a horizontal line in red crayon all the way around the rustic Chinese wallpaper in the dining room.

The wallpaper had scenes of big willow trees bent charmingly over placid ponds stretching into the distance and graceful bamboo bridges over little canals with sweet birds flying overhead two by two. To my way of thinking, the red line was hardly noticeable and not really ruining anything.

"What's this?" Mother screamed as she walked in from the party. "Abby, have you been writing in the dining room?"

Various stages of rage cascaded from Mother. First there was discovery, then shock that the Chinese countryside had been defaced.

"What have you done? All the way around the dining room? You've ruined it."

Then came her demands for an immediate and total surrender. She wanted a confession.

"Why did you do this? Why?" She grabbed my arms and shook, hard. "What made you do this?"

In retrospect, it would have been smart to cut my losses and confess right then. But the climate in the house wasn't generating rational thought. Also, I had no idea how important the beautiful dining room was to her; its charm gave her pleasure and peace. And besides, I didn't know how to answer her: I didn't know why I'd done it.

"Maybe," I said, "since I had the crayon in my pocket and I walked along the wall, maybe it rubbed off on the wall!" I shrugged. "Maybe that's what happened."

No dice.

She called Daddy at his office and demanded that he come home to deliver discipline. Then she grabbed me, sat me down on the stairs. "You wait right there, young lady, until he comes home," she said. "We'll see what he has to say."

"Hit her," she bellowed as soon as he came across the threshold. His expression was curious and cautious. "She's ruined the dining room and needs a good whipping," she shrieked.

Daddy, looking ashen, rolled up *The New York Times,* and after a few moments hit me gently on the backside.

My daddy did that.

I escaped his grasp and ran past him, up the wooden staircase that seemed longer and steeper than ever. I ran into my bedroom closet—way back to a dark crawl space where

I could huddle with my shame. After fifteen, maybe twenty minutes, I was used to the dark, and I began to realize I was *persona non grata* everywhere but in the closet. Just as I started to consider my options, Mother called in a voice that put the false in falsetto, "Come down. It's time for dinner."

And that was that. No one talked about it. I don't remember the dinner conversation, but I remember the look on Daddy's face. Fifty years later, a friendly therapist from South Africa explained his expression—that it wasn't because he hated me, but that he was pained because his wife had put him in a situation in which he'd been driven to hit his little girl. "Most pediatricians," she told me in her cultivated accent, "think that hitting a young child is counterproductive, you know."

There are a couple of comments in defense of my mother to be added here. She didn't understand what I needed, and I didn't know how to explain it. She craved beauty and elegance, and I craved hugs and kisses.

On another occasion, sometime after I'd started ballet lessons, I decided to put on a performance of *Swan Lake* for visiting aunts. I dressed in my pale green tulle skirt adorned with red silk roses that I'd worn for my recital, completing the outfit with my new red leather ballet slippers. Carried away with enthusiasm (I always loved a performance), I set up the portable record player and borrowed (without permission) my mother's exquisite hand mirror with a silver back. After all, what's *Swan Lake* without a lake? At the impassioned crescendo of the music, I put my red-slippered foot onto the center of the mirror and—*voilà!*—the mirror crunched. Splitsville! All the old biddies in their velvet hats and shining brooches who were watching in a row from the brown silk couch gasped in unison.

Not wanting this wretched detail to stop the performance, I ran the broken mirror to the sidelines, turned the music louder, and continued. Mother clearly wasn't happy. But since the aunts were there, she put on her "I'm a good sport" façade.

Later, trying to temper her obvious exasperation, she smiled at me and asked, "What made you do that?"

I didn't know what to say. *Who knew the mirror would break?*

At times like this, in her moments of frustration with the downs of motherhood, Mother would go to her beloved piano and play Chopin. It was an escape to her world of grace and romance. She'd lift her slender wrists above the keys, and I'd watch her fingers dance as she swayed from side to side at her Steinway. The honeyed bravado of a polonaise probably transported her from her duties of motherhood into the world of the imagination. The music she played was always beautiful. It filled the room with cotton candy romance.

MOTHER'S ADVICE

Music was always important to Mother. She had majored in music at Wellesley College (Class of 1929). She'd even written her class's marching song, which she sang with great pride and taught both her daughters to do the same.

> As we march to the sound of our voices
> No matter what time it may be
> We will fervently sing Wellesley's praises
> In a voice that is joyous and free.
> Wellesley! Wellesley! Wellesley '29!

Sex advice, on the other hand, wasn't her strong suit. (N.B.: Mother was born in 1907—thirteen years before women had the right to vote. Few women born in 1907 were speaking about sexual satisfaction with their daughters.) Mother summoned her daughters separately to approach her bedroom for the so-called advice. She sat on her bed in a fluffy white negligee, knees up with her back propped against two pillows and a *Vogue* magazine in front of her. She said, "You're old enough now to understand that when you're dating, you have to be very responsible. The most important thing is not to be intimate. You should wait until you're married." Then she repeated the four-word dictum: "Just don't get pregnant."

Up to this point, I had some idea of how sex worked, although my girlfriends didn't offer much information. Betsy was so dainty I wouldn't even mention it. Sandra was more adventuresome; she put her middle finger straight in the air to demonstrate her boyfriend's progress in sexual exploration. Marilyn was going to clue me in on her adventures, and I was anxious for the news. But her grandmother kept coming into the room, dashing my hopes for more details.

"I have a good book of information. Would you like that?" queried my mother.

"No. I know what I have to know." I smiled sheepishly. "I've talked it over with my girlfriends."

"Do you have any questions?" she asked.

I didn't want her to think I was a dumb bunny, so I asked, "Is it like putting a plug into a socket?"

"Go to your room," she bellowed.

So much for my sex education.

There was another piece of information she tried to imprint on my young mind. "You know," she said several times, "you can fall in love with a rich boy just as easily as you can fall in love with a poor one."

I was a sophomore at Wellesley College when that advice became particularly dispiriting.

The plan was that Daddy, Mother, and I would go to the Bridgeport, Connecticut, railroad station after my weekend visit home, and I would transfer from one train to another to get to Wellesley.

I bought my ticket and stood with them on the desolate track platform. The train whistle sounded in the distance. It probably motivated Mother to think this was the last opportunity to run the rich-boy propaganda by me for a while. She grabbed my arm. "Just remember, whatever you do, Abby, don't come home with a poor schmo."

I pulled away and walked down the platform to avoid her. Daddy came toward me with a poker face. He looked at me for a few seconds, then at Mother, then back at me. "I just want you to know," he said, loud enough for Mother to hear him, "that since Mother won't be happy with a poor schmo, I won't be happy with a rich schmo."

He paused and pursed his lips. His mustache looked funny when he did that, and I couldn't help but smile. "Do you know why, Abby?" he asked.

"No. I don't know why, Daddy."

"Well, you have to answer a riddle to find out."

I noticed that Mother was gradually inching toward us.

"What's the riddle?"

"What's the difference between a rich schmo and a poor schmo?"

"I don't know. What *is* the difference between a rich schmo and a poor schmo?"

"Nothing. A schmo. Is a schmo. Is a schmo."

I laughed. Daddy stood there, still with that poker face, but now also with a twinkle in his eye. Even Mother laughed. I shook my head, grabbed my suitcase, and headed for the train and college.

As soon as I arrived at my dorm, Mother called. "Are you OK?"

I knew she regretted her abrasive tone. "Yeah, I'm OK. But I don't want to talk now," I replied, exhausted by our inability to come together.

On many occasions Daddy's remarks brought laughter, inspiration, or relief to our lives. For instance, as he grew older he suffered from a condition that made his esophagus become narrower and eating more difficult. He decided to train himself to stretch his esophagus like sword-swallowers do. Twice a week he swallowed rubber tubes with weights at the bottom and pulled them out of his esophagus to keep it from shrinking. He had two tubes, a small one he called "Baby" and a wider one he named "Big Boy." He told me that as he approached the sink in the bathroom to swallow and bring up the tubes, he would instruct them both, "Baby and Big Boy, now don't give me any trouble today."

Later still, I had the sad task of encouraging Daddy to move to a more institutional part of his apartment complex, where he could receive nursing care. "Daddy, both your daughters love you," I said gently, "and we think it would be better if you could move to the nursing wing." I was expecting to get some gentle argument in return. But he smiled at me and said, "When two people tell you you're drunk, it's time to lie down."

When he was eighty, he experienced a nasty fall. "Daddy, what did you do after you fell?" I asked.

He thought for a minute and replied, "I asked myself: What can I do to help myself now?"

PART TWO

COLLEGE DAYS

WELLESLEY

I always knew Wellesley was a place of excellence with high educational standards. Yet I kept thinking that my college days were the only opportunity for me to be charming, wear nice clothes, and find a mate. With that attitude, it's no wonder most of the classes at Wellesley weren't arresting.

Take, for example, Professor Sullivan's Modern History class, which we called "Egypt to Eisenhower." Forty young women would file two or three times a week into an amphitheater, where Mr. Sullivan appeared with a pile of note cards. He would read from the top card and, having finished, would carefully flip the card over, thereby beginning a second pile of note cards. Before he read from the next card, he would straighten out both piles. His hands assiduously tapped the sides of the piles to make sure the one he'd just flipped was stacked exactly on top of the one below. While all the other girls were taking notes based on his oratory, I was keeping track of the note cards: one pile growing exponentially and the other dwindling into nothing. I didn't know what education was about, but I was sure it should be more engaging than watching Mr. Sullivan's note cards.

As a general rule, in my other courses I did as little assigned reading as possible and hoped I wouldn't be called upon to sound informed. Philosophy was particularly maddening because I could find no philosophical treatise that answered as many questions as it raised.

English Composition was difficult because I didn't know how to grapple with a strange vocabulary. One day at the beginning of class, the instructor asked if there were any words in the assignment we didn't understand. I raised my hand (I was being honest) and asked what *erotic* meant. The instructor looked at me strangely and asked if I knew who Eros was. When I said I did, he told me, "Just use your imagination." I thought about Eros, that cherub with fat thighs, tiny wings, a sweet smile, and a bow and arrow. I was surprised that the cherub had anything to do with sex, but I took the teacher at his word.

I also had difficulty with my Bible professor. Studying the Bible seemed intense with this professor, and a group of girls adored him. One of his assignments was to write an essay defining "biography." I wrote that it was one man's opinion of another man's worth. I received a D on the essay. After class he told me that "biography" was a *communication* between two people and that my answer lacked depth. I never joined the group of girls who adored the Bible professor.

As time went on, I decided that if I could explore a topic on my own and choose what to read, college would be more fun.

I made an appointment to see my major advisor, the chairman of the history department, to ask permission for independent study. He gazed at me over his reading spectacles as if I was disturbing his rest and said, "Your history grades, Miss Bogin, are not high enough to merit independent study."

"But if I could work on something that really interested me, I might get a higher grade."

"What really interests you, Miss Bogin?"

It's a long shot. But what the heck? "I would like to write a paper contrasting Thomas Jefferson and Thomas Paine."

Pause. The chairman of the history department at Wellesley was not convinced. "If you can find *anyone* in the history department who is willing to be your advisor, you may do it."

I knew one professor, a friendly guy, who I thought might be enthusiastic. When he asked me why I chose that topic, I said, "Well, both men contributed to the era. One had an elegant life in Paris, while the other guy, also talented, was pretty lonely. Especially when he died." He must have liked that idea. He told me to submit a bibliography within two days and, after reviewing my ambitious list, immediately signed the form that granted me official permission to pursue independent study.

I loved the work. I read all the sources in my bibliography and threw in two additional pamphlets. I received an A-/B+ on the final paper about these two towering figures of the eighteenth century: the slave-owning gentleman who died at his beloved estate, Monticello, his home set on five thousand Virginia acres, and his contemporary whose words rallied the troops in Valley Forge and died a forgotten man in Greenwich Village, New York.

At Wellesley I became president of the Shakespeare Society. My friend Sara Jane had mounted a successful electoral campaign, spreading the word that I would devote myself to the Bard and to the upkeep of the little Elizabethan house we treasured. We put on festive performances and a dinner in the house in honor of Shakespeare's birthday. I played Theseus, Duke of Athens, in a rollicking all-girl's performance of *A Midsummer Night's Dream.* Shakespeare's imaginative, bewitching language was getting deep into my soul.

There were other things about Wellesley that made me happy. The colorful instructor Paul Barstow ignited my love of theatre. I met him one day quite by accident in the library, after returning from my first job interview.

"How are you, Abby?" Mr. Barstow asked me.

"I'm terrible. I just came back from an interview at Little, Brown and Company. Now I realize that if I got a job there, I'd have to sit at a desk all day after college. I'd rather die."

"Would you like to go to graduate school at Yale School of Drama?" he asked.

Wow. That could be fun. … Daddy went to Yale. … How bad could it be? I love plays and performances. … And besides, there are lots of boys there. I might find someone to marry.

"Sure," I replied.

"Well, get an application, fill it out, and send it in. I'll write a letter of recommendation for you, honey." Which he did. And the following academic year I felt like I'd gone from a closet to a grand ballroom.

However, the most important player in my college years was a certain "gentleman" caller.

THE "GENTLEMAN" CALLER

On a quiet Sunday afternoon in Beebee Hall, the seedy mansion in the Quad where Mother had lived before me, the student in charge of greeting visitors at the front door announced that I had a gentleman caller.

I went down the dark, wide oak staircase in the college dorm to see no one I knew. But there, with his arm nonchalantly propped up against a pillar, his body in a lovely *contrapposto,* all relaxed but strong, stood a young man. He was short— about my father's height. He watched my every move as I descended the stairs, assessing my legs, my breasts, my hair, my very being.

"Uh-oh," he said as he watched. "Uh-oh, uh-oh, uh-oh. Shoot. Am I in trouble now. I knew it when I looked at this fool book." He waved the freshman directory in my direction, his copy rolled up and frayed despite its being recently printed. "I knew just from this little picture of you," now wagging his finger at me, but with a big smile, "I was in *deep trouble.*"

His Southern drawl was mixed with ever so delightful mischief and a totally phony but captivating helplessness.

"My mama went to Wellesley," he continued, "and she told me some Northern belle would steal my heart a lot sooner than a Southern lady from Atlanta." Coming from his mouth, the second *t* sound in *Atlanta* didn't exist because his accent softened the language. "Oh, am I in trouble now."

My heart was beating fast. He was so cute. I loved his massive neck and shoulders, his light brown hair, his scholarly glasses (so at odds with his physical charisma), and, most of all, that mischief. I'd never witnessed such charm: What a game he had—such play, such phony, self-effacing boldness. It was delicious.

He wore chinos, a blue oxford shirt open at the neck, and white buck shoes. Because he was so bold and in control, I could think of nothing to do but play it straight. I pretended to ignore all his outrageous puffery and flattery, which I was actually loving.

"I don't know you," I told him. "But my mother went to Wellesley too. What class was your mother?"

"Mama was '34." He looked at me like a fox about to get into the chicken coop.

I acted like I was above such crass behavior. "What was your mother's name? My mother talks a lot about how it was when she was here."

He pulled out his wallet and said, "Here's a picture of my mama from the Atlanta newspaper … where she has meetings with all her little Wellesley ladies. She's done this so, so-o-o-o long she herself is the Atlanta Wellesley Club. … Am I glad to see you. I'm Sam Elger and I'm at Harvard." He motioned with his head in what I supposed was the direction of Harvard.

I loved his casual air, his control of the moment, and what I imagined were his strong thighs under those preppy pants. Most of all, I was thrilled about the way he made a fuss over me. Yet I acted like I didn't care.

"What's your major?" I asked.

"Honey, I'm pre-med and all shook up."

Mother likes doctors, and so do I.

"Uh-huh. I'm gonna call you soon and we'll go drinking with my buddies and the girls. OK, honey?"

"How do I know who you are? I mean, you could be anybody."

"Oh, oh. You little fussbudget." He looked heavenward and smiled as he got closer to me. He pulled out his wallet again. "Well, honey, here's my driver's license. You see I'm from Atlanta. And here's my Harvard meal ticket. And here's my membership in the Andover Alumni Club. I've been North for some time, honey. You see you're looking at a legitimate fella. … Your mama would approve."

You're damn right. I looked away and tried to hide how hot I felt. The soft glow of the early September dusk was all around us as I walked him out the door to the deep-green field in front of the dorm.

We stood together by a huge beech tree and then walked in perfect harmony around the limbs bent to the ground with handsome green leaves. The wind was soft, the light golden as if on cue from the afternoon sun.

"I'm calling you real soon, honey." He stood perfectly still, looked deep into my eyes, and chuckled. He didn't touch me. And yet I was captured by Mother's dreams and his overwhelming charm.

For the next two years we spoke on the phone once a week, saw one another most weekends. We weren't part of the sexually active high jinks on campuses. But Sam did get drunk most Saturday nights and I would tag along: the Smiling Enabler.

UH-OH

I was hoping it was going to be an ordinary summer weekend. But I'd had an intimation that something would go wrong days before, when Lucy was the only pal who was free to be my guest that weekend. I always wanted friends to share my visits home. It alleviated my feeling of desperation about not being married—or even on the way to being married.

This was a lonely time for me because Sam and I had dated for two years and he still hadn't asked me to marry him. But my rationale was that anyone that adorable was worth waiting for. He fulfilled all my mother's criteria for a mate: well-off family, right schools, good mind, and devilishly charming. I loved the same things in him. I knew he cared about me, and I figured if I just waited he'd eventually ask to marry me. So there had been a lot of groping and stroking instead of love, a lot of football weekends with drunken buddies instead of honest conversation. Then he went away to medical school after he finished Harvard, and I waited around at Wellesley for him to change his mind.

Lucy and I arrived home that weekend, and I felt the usual desperation. I was grateful for Lucy's pointless chatter. When we brought in our suitcases, Mother, with a sly smile, handed me my mail. A letter from Sam was on top. I left Lucy in the kitchen, encouraging her to have a cold drink, and went into the dining room to delight in his letter.

On the envelope appeared his usual scruffy handwriting, which I treasured.

"Dear Abby," the letter began. "It's time for me to write about what is happening to me now. Although you and I have shared many times and a lot of memories, my friendship with Annie has grown into love, and we plan to marry in the near future. Although she knows I have an unusual loyalty to you, she knows I love her. I wish you good luck in your life ahead and know that you will have a fine future. Sincerely, Sam."

I read it again and again. I looked hard at the piece of paper and his big, distinctive scrawl. A cold ache went from my stomach to my shoulders. My mouth had gone dry. My ears rang with a stinging, muffled din. In fact, I felt like I was wrapped up in a rug.

"Hi," I said with a smile when I finally returned to Lucy. "Look, I have a very important letter to go over with my parents. So do you mind hanging out in my room till we're done?"

She smiled and followed me, lugging her suitcase up the stairs. I told her I'd come back when I was through and shut the door.

I walked down the dark wooden stairs again, with weak legs and a pounding head. Mother and Daddy were in the den. "There's something I have to tell you," I said, shutting the double doors with both hands.

I turned around to look at them. Mother was lying down on the couch, wrapped like a mummy in the heavy woolen afghan she'd knitted. My guess was that the blanket's warmth and tightness gave her comfort. Daddy was seated on the opposite couch, his body relaxed, legs crossed, one arm stretched easily over the back of the couch, the other around a rolled copy of *The New York Times.*

"Sam has written to tell me he's marrying a girl he knows from medical school. They're getting married soon. It's all over between us."

Quiet. Then Mother moaned. "Call him," she implored. "Don't let him do this." She was feeling my pain. "Try to get him back."

I turned to Daddy, desperately seeking help. He looked into my eyes. He smiled that gentle, steady smile. There was a long pause before he spoke. "Thank God that's over." As Mother's eyes darted around the room, he continued to look straight at me, his eyes unwavering.

I'm bobbing in the ocean with rolling waves; I'm helpless in the churning sea. I'm going to drown. Daddy has thrown me a life preserver, a huge round white O on a thick nautical line. I grab hold and know I won't drown.

I looked back at him and said, "Yes, it's over and there's nothing left to do. I think I'll go find Lucy."

I left the room, climbed the stairs again, my legs still weak, and thanked Lucy for letting me finish the important business with my parents. I opened the closet in my bedroom and the top drawer in my little brown dresser full of affectionate letters, funny birthday cards, and souvenirs from Sam. I put his last letter on top. I looked closely at the pile of envelopes and slowly closed the drawer. I didn't cry because Lucy was there. I didn't moan because Mother moaned. I simply turned to Lucy and said, "Let's eat."

Many years later Daddy was sick and in the hospital. I told him then and again later how he'd saved me when I felt I was drowning—and that his response to the whole Sam debacle had been like throwing me a life preserver.

Even in his sickness, he was able to smile that same steady smile he'd showed me at the moment my fantasy had been snuffed.

PART THREE

COUPLING 101

MOTHER MAY BE DOWN, BUT SHE'S NOT OUT

I figured Mother was spending a lot of time curled up in her big brown afghan, worrying about her not married but marriageable daughter. Yet, as it turned out, Mother might have been down, but she was definitely not out.

The annual Apple Festival at the Aspetuck Valley Apple Barn in Easton, Connecticut, was on, and the scent of the big hay barn's dirt floor and the sweet smell of apples in pies, cakes, croissants, and cookies made the forty minutes' travel worthwhile.

It was impossible for a Fairfield County resident to miss out on the twenty-odd rows of bushel baskets stretching across the middle of the barn. Signs displayed the origin and name of each type of apple: Red Delicious, Golden Delicious, Macintosh, Braeburn, Cortland, Honeycrisp, Winesap, Rhode Island Greening, and Gravenstein. And with maple sugar candy, maple syrup, peanut brittle, and applesauce added to the mix, customers of every age were happy. There was an old-fashioned cider mill still operational, as well as giant brown plastic pails that held bunches of black-eyed Susans and even a few dislocated-looking sunflowers.

Mother reported to me later that the following had transpired over the Honeycrisps.

She, mother of Abby, the marriageable daughter, and Miriam, sister of Ken, the marriageable bachelor surgeon, spotted one another. They were from the same town and knew each other. Two sets of probing eyes amid apples, exchanging pleasantries, both with the same hidden agenda.

"Oh, hello," said Mother. "How are you?"

"Just fine," said Miriam. "What brings you so far out to the country?"

"I know you can buy these apples in town. But nothing is as good as Aspetuck!" said the first.

"Oh, yes. I agree. And nothing is so nice as this good country air," said the other.

Mother reported that she and Miriam eyed each other carefully. Although Miriam was dedicated to piano recitals in town, she was younger and not part of Mother's crowd. But the two women had something in common on this particular day.

Mother laughed when she reported the conversation to me.

She asked Miriam, "How is your brother?"

Miriam smiled, looked directly at Mother, and said, "How's your daughter?"

The two arranged for the daughter and brother to meet since they were both in Boston—I, designing theatrical costumes until school started again, and Ken, finishing his surgical training.

Our courtship began in Boston.

He called me and we went out for a quick dinner one Saturday before he had to go back to work.

On the second date a few days later, he guided my elbow as we crossed the street.

Oh my god. He's handsome and smart. And if I can catch him, I will.

Ken probably was thinking, "She has the same lively eyes as Mama. And she's spunky."

A week later I waited for Ken on the red brick steps of my apartment on Commonwealth Avenue. I wore my favorite purple silk shirt and tried to look casual in jeans and sneakers.

I watched Ken's solid frame as he swaggered down the avenue in a farmer's plaid shirt and jeans, carrying a brown paper bag full of big, ripe Bing cherries. He would eat one, pause, and then joyfully spit out the pit, shooting it as far in front of him as he could. Each pit became a missile. Ken would make a funny *thoom* sound with each launching. He would watch the pit fall, proud of the distance, and then eat another cherry.

I watched his progress down the street. *He's different from any other guy I've ever met. He's a funny duck. Not boring.*

Our dates were always rushed. After I returned to school, I would go back to Boston to stay with friends and see Ken when he finished rounds late Saturday. Or he would come to Connecticut, stay with his mom, and leave early Sunday to make rounds before the Monday Grand Rounds.

Ken made each date fun. We visited a colleague in the Massachusetts countryside and stopped on the way to make friends with a little lost yearling. We sailed with friends in a rented sailboat on the Connecticut shore. Then there were Ken's favorite ethnic restaurants in Boston, where I learned to love baba ganoush, falafel, and General Tso's chicken. By August we were engaged.

Once when I came to Boston, we sat down at a tiny round cocktail table in a dark bar on a Saturday right. He had just finished his shift. Ken immediately lit up a Marlboro and breathed in deeply, shaking off his fatigue.

I kissed his ear and grabbed his hand. "You've just showered, right? You smell like a whole bar of Lifebuoy." I kissed him again. "On you it smells good. … How was work?"

"New low today," he muttered. "I put my head into a new incubator to see what it was like. They'd just brought them onto the floor. You know what happened? I fell asleep! There! On my feet! I fell asleep with my head in the incubator and my feet on the floor."

"Are you OK now?"

"I'm fine. And I'm gonna order. I've been here before. We're going for snails and French bread. And I know just the wine for snails. Pouilly-Fuissé. It's my favorite. You'll love it."

"Sounds great."

Suddenly he was concentrating on the pepper shaker. "Abby, I've been thinking about us. Maybe we should slow down … let some time go by. I'm just not sure about our plans."

I cleared my throat. *Oh boy. Oh boy. He's getting away. He's got cold feet. Listen, Abby, if you ever needed to talk good, the time is NOW. Go for it.*

I looked into Ken's eyes and grabbed his arm. "Honey, it's very normal to be unsure. This is a big commitment, and we're both in a new place. But usually the thing that worries you isn't the thing that turns out to be bad." *Pause here, kid.* "You'll be fine. It's totally normal to be worried. You wouldn't be human if you weren't worried. I'm sure you and I are going to be fine once we get used to being married." I gave him a gracious smile and rubbed his arm.

Ken looked at me. He was quiet. "OK. Maybe you're right. … But I had to tell you what I was thinking." He hesitated, and I kept rubbing his arm and smiling. I stayed very still. Then his face brightened. "I had to tell you my worries," he continued. "I feel better now. Hey. Let's forget the wine. This is so important, we need champagne! This is a moment to remember!"

He's overreacting, that's for sure. It's a little crazy, but I'll go along with whatever works.

TWO DINNERS

On a sunny day in August, Ken and Mother were driving around together, hunting for a place for our wedding reception in the estate area of Southport, Connecticut. I was to join them shortly.

Ken reported to me later that they slowed down in front of a two-hundred-year-old sea captain's mansion. A spreading beech tree stood in front.

A tall man in white trousers and a bright green silk jacket came outside. He wore a silk foulard ascot at his throat, with a matching handkerchief casually stuffed into his breast pocket. He was blond, slim, and, judging from his gait, in good shape.

As they stopped to gaze at the scene, Mother looked at the man then turned to Ken, comfy in jeans and a sloppy sweater, and said, "That's the kind of man I always thought Abby would marry." Ken had been admiring the beech tree. Now his future mother-in-law's observation pulled his attention to what she was looking at.

Ken looked at the man and then his future mother-in-law and chuckled. As he saw an improbable dream revealed, he began to laugh. Mother, nettled by his response, drew up her disciplined frame, smart in lavender silk, and grew annoyed. That made him laugh even harder.

There it was: The thorny relationship between Mother, who yearned for a life of Anglo-Saxon elegance, and Ken, the immigrant's handsome son, energetic and happy in his own skin.

As soon as we were engaged, Ken's mother asked Ken and me to join her for Shabbos dinner. Anna was a petite, energetic Russian émigrée with a rock-solid belief in God and His might. Her house was a tiny square suburban box, set on a tiny square suburban lot by a tiny stream she called the Rooster River. No one knew why she'd always called it the Rooster River. But my guess was that she, who felt very much at home in the wilderness, liked to think that her house still resembled the farmlands she'd loved in northern Connecticut. That's where she had buried an eight-day-old infant who died of jaundice, raised four more kids, and adored the work that went into tending chickens and a cow, sewing and cleaning, keeping kosher and praying on Friday night and Saturday morning. Her husband, Morris, long since dead, had a different sensibility: He was an intellectual whose only close friend in town had been the local parish priest. (They both knew Hebrew and discussed which parts of the Bible made sense.)

The table Anna prepared that night bespoke her love of work and God. The linen tablecloth was worn but starched and ironed. Everything shined. Instead of two brass candlesticks that would have been appropriate for a Shabbos celebration, Anna had five. In the mellow light of the evening, they shined like gold. Each of us had a small braided challah, glowing where melted butter had been painted on the top, right from the oven. The greatest shine came from Anna's face because she delighted in her children, cleaning the objects that gave Shabbos its special meaning, and saying the prayers.

After dinner Ken drove me back to my parents' house then proceeded to Boston and work.

As soon as I got home, I was surrounded with Mother's sadness. She was lying down on the couch in the den, rolled up in her big brown afghan.

Ken returned the next weekend for dinner at my parents' house. Mother had Rose, our family cook and friend, prepare the usual golden chicken, baked crisp in orange juice with wedges of lemon, broiled baby asparagus, and Southern corn pudding. The table was set with fine crystal and silver. Dessert was a study in color: slices of pale green honeydew with scoops of raspberry sorbet and sprigs of mint, served in a small crystal bowl for each of us.

Daddy looked at Ken and said, "Welcome to the family. Let's drink to a happy and healthy life for the two of you." He raised his glass of white wine and expected us to do the same.

After Ken touched glasses with Daddy, he stood and said in a loud, celebratory voice, "L'chaim, l'chaim, if ve don't beat 'em, at least v'ill tie 'em!" Mother cringed at Ken's ebullient Yiddish accent. But Daddy chuckled because it reminded him of bygone days with his beloved grandfather. Ken and Daddy, both physicians and good-humored men, were very much at home with each other, and they proceeded to drink several glasses of wine and share Jewish jokes.

"What's the difference between a schlemiel and a shlimazl?" asked Ken.

"Well," Daddy answered, "a schlemiel drops a piece of toast on the floor butter side UP, but a schlimazl drops a piece of toast on the floor butter side DOWN."

"Boys, boys," said Mother. "Please. Let's eat before the chicken gets cold!" She was interrupting steadily increasing gaiety.

"Dad, I have another one for you," said Ken, enjoying the boldness of the moment. "A schlemiel is somebody who spills his soup. A schlimazel is the guy it lands on!"

"I haven't heard that one before! Very good, Ken. More wine?"

"Sure-lee!" said Ken. The wine was good, and Ken's Yiddish accent is getting thicker and louder. "Here's one maybe you haven't heard before. Feinstein comes back from a business trip to find that his wife has been fooling around. 'Who was it? That creep Epstein?'

"'No,' says the wife.

"'Was it that jerk Levy?'

"'No,' says the wife.'"

By now Ken had stood up and assumed the role of Feinstein. "'I know. It must have been that idiot Hymie.'

"'No,' says the wife.'

"'What's the matter?'" Ken/Feinstein yelled, at the top of his Yiddish anger. "'None of my friends are good enough for you?'"

Now it was crystal clear that Mother's dreams and Ken's energies were bilious together. I wasn't keen on Ken's showing off either. But his jokes *were* funny, and dinner otherwise would have been tense and stuffy.

The meal went by quickly, with Ken singing a fine rendition of Tom Lehrer's "Vatican Rag":

> First you get down on your knees,
> Fiddle with your rosaries,
> Bow your head with great respect,
> And genuflect, genuflect, genuflect!

I thought that was funny. But by the time Ken yelled his last humdinger at the door -"Hey, Mabel - get off the table. The two bucks is for the beer," I was relieved that he was leaving. We briefly kissed goodnight, he left to catch a train to Boston and work, and I went to sleep.

I woke up at 2 AM, consumed with the thought that a union of my mother's elegance and my fiancé's crude comedy wasn't going to work. I didn't know what to do.

I got out of bed to talk to my parents. As I saw my hand reach for the doorknob, I felt like I was caught in the middle of an Alfred Hitchcock movie.

Then I stopped and drew my hand away. *It's stupid to ask them if I should marry Ken. They can't get inside my skin. They can't see him through my eyes. The only one who knows whether this marriage should take place is me. Just go back to bed and think it over.*

I pictured the two mothers at dinner—Anna, with her ability to find joy, and Edith, with her sadness. I thought about Ken's vitality, his brains, and his happy strength and decided to go through with the wedding.

KEN OPERATES

Once I made the decision to marry Ken, he became my hero. He emanated more energy and optimism than any other man I knew.

I asked him if I could see him operate. He arranged for me to view a procedure from a room with a glass floor above a surgical theatre in a teaching hospital in Boston.

Eight people—students, I assumed—were seated around the perimeter of the viewing room. When I first saw Ken walk in with his purposeful stride, my heart leaped. Although he looked lost in woefully oversized scrubs, he was my man. I had a clear view of the quiet and seemingly airless operating room: two surgeons, four nurses, one tiny infant patient, and two tables with instruments laid in orderly rows. The sleeping baby had pallid, grey skin and six tubes poking out of his body. Ken was speaking to the surgeon across from him. The fellow listened intently. Ken seemed to be giving instructions; when the other surgeon nodded, Ken began. He looked to be splitting the baby's chest in half, and I was astonished at the speed and deliberateness with which he worked. When he asked for an instrument, he poked his hand behind him and the nurse put it forcefully into his palm. Although I couldn't see inside the baby, I knew Ken was correcting his tiny heart.

Ninety minutes later Ken moved away from the table and the operation seemed over. Four tubes were removed, bloody sheets were dumped in bins, and the baby, looking pinkish now, with none of that strange grey color, was wheeled out.

After seeing an actual operation, I had a different understanding of what Ken had chosen to do with his life. I had thought of surgery in superficialities, as if it were television drama. Witnessing a real procedure led me to understand how rigorous and demanding Ken's profession was and how precious it would be to someone who needed him. Ken could make parents and offspring whole again in a world where tragedy was painful and abundant. He had a talent for it.

Later I learned that if kids were very frightened when entering his office for an examination, Ken would get on the floor to play with blocks or rings with them. Once he played like this with an autistic child for an hour, and while they played Ken examined him. The child kissed Ken goodbye, which the mom reported the boy had never done before.

As Ken and I grew closer over the years, I was touched to hear him talking to parents of sick kids on the phone. "Call me anytime," he would say. "Every question is a good one. I'm here for you," he would say over and over again. I was aware that those words were helping people in deep distress. "I'm here for you. I'm here for you."

Sometimes the phone would ring in the middle of the night. He would get out of bed very quickly to make sure he got the details of the case—as if he knew that by standing at attention he could absorb information more clearly. I guessed that this was how he'd responded to emergencies when he was in training. He seemed to wipe everything else out of his mind and focus all his attention on the task at hand. As he got dressed, I would hurry to make coffee for him. I'd also offer him toast, but he never took it, saying, "No, no," in a gentle way as he quickly headed out into the dark for the hospital.

Many times we had to cancel dinners and postpone plans with the kids, and that was OK because the patient mattered first. I wanted to support Ken because he was so good at what he did and his goal was so precious.

CLANG

When Ken said, "Let's get married" in early August of 1963, I replied, smiling, "Sure."

From then until the wedding on October 29, I was so frightened I felt I was locked in an out-of-body experience. (Years later my son Matthew described this "precipice moment" in one's life clearly and definitively, as was his wont: "I don't want to *get* married," said my son. "I just want to *be* married.")

When I called my college buddy Catia to give her the news that I was marrying soon, she asked, "Is he worthy of you?" I didn't know what to say because I had no idea.

Mother and I made wedding decisions quickly. I would wear my sister's bridal dress—it wasn't my style, but that was easier than finding a new one. The flowers, because the wedding was to have an autumnal theme, would be informal bouquets of deep gold Shasta daisies and blazing gold black-eyed Susans. We decided on bridesmaids and two pudgy little tykes as flower girls who, it turned out, carried their fancy florist's bouquets with lovable disregard.

Ken named his groomsmen and best man. Since he wasn't around, having secured time off for the honeymoon by working with no days off, I ordered the rental jackets for them. Daddy's and Ken's jackets measured the same. That was one of the few factoids I found reassuring.

Mother and I traveled to New York City for an engagement photo at the studio of Bradford Bachrach, a well-known society photographer. We took a late train and barely got to the studio in time. I sat for thirty minutes in a cavernous and chilly room. Mother waited on the sidelines as the photographer's assistant posed me and adjusted floodlights by dragging a step stool from one light pole to another, twisting knobs, and running up and down the stool. Mother reminded me to sit up straight and rearranged my new pearl necklace. I felt clammy and hungry. Under the lights in the cavernous room, I gave way eventually, slid out of the chair, and fainted onto the floor.

The assistant ran for smelling salts and a matron. Mother looked horrified and asked for hot tea and a biscuit, since I hadn't eaten breakfast. In a jiffy, the actual photographer appeared, a calm man who was the only reassuring person in the room. He smiled and helped me up from the floor. Four biscuits and two cups of tea later I was ready for my close-up. The photographer looked at me reassuringly. He said he would take the photograph we needed in record time and that it would be lovely. I wore a wishy-washy smile in the photo; it was certainly not the photographer's fault.

Two years earlier, when I thought I was likely to cry at the sweetness and solemnity of my sister's wedding, I had asked Daddy for advice. "Well, Abby," he'd replied, "whenever you feel you're going to cry, just remember how much the flowers, the champagne, the luncheon at the Birchwood Country Club, the music, and the wedding cake are going to cost. Think of a cash register going *CLANG*, then say '*CLANG*' and you won't cry."

My day bloomed bright and cheerful enough, and Daddy and I laughed at our plan to keep the *CLANG* method reinstituted for my own wedding. Several times during that out-of-body experience, Daddy and I looked at one another and whispered, "*CLANG*" to keep fear under control. It worked every time.

Ken and I honeymooned in the Caribbean and then moved into a little walk-up in Boston so he could complete his surgical training. I withdrew from Yale Drama School with some regret, but I continued my theatre studies at Boston University to be near my new husband. The university, in my opinion, didn't offer the gifted instructors I'd found at Yale, yet the study continued to fascinate me.

We were young and in love and excited to think of a long road trip to the West Coast, heading out to explore the Grand Canyon, the great desert, and the John Muir Trail on our way.

Once Ken had decided on one more year of study specifically in pediatric surgery, I asked him why. He was silent for several minutes and then quietly said, "Kids are better people."

"What do you mean?"

"They tell you the truth. They know what matters. And they're not phony."

He says a lot of beautiful things, and that was one of them.

PART FOUR

COUPLING 201

LETTER WRITING

What lay ahead showed a different side of the man.

Ken had graduated from Harvard Medical School, trained in Boston's famous teaching hospitals, and completed his training in pediatric surgery on the West Coast.

His plan was to get accepted for surgical privileges in a hospital of his choice, and then begin his surgical career. He assumed that his good grades and letters of recommendation from former bosses would get him those privileges. We wanted to find a city we liked—we were considering Tucson, Philadelphia, and Baltimore, apply for Ken's privileges, and move right in.

We were optimistic and almost giddy. *Ken is through studying!* He had mastered the techniques he needed to begin the work he loved. We looked forward to driving across the country and settling down. Every morning we'd plot the day's schedule while we ate in some diner where the local fare delighted us: slabs of corned beef hash with an oozing poached egg, or hominy grits with thick slices of bacon, or stacks of pancakes drizzled with strawberries and confectioner's sugar.

Ken had planned a route that included stops in the three cities we favored. He'd contacted the chief of surgery in each city and had had records and recommendations sent ahead. But as we traveled, the plan began to have problems. We would meet the surgeon and listen while he discussed his own hospital's needs and how Ken might fit in. What we thought would be positive news was turning out to be disappointing. Every surgeon told us there was no opening and that we should look down the road.

> "Hello, my boy. You have a fine record. I know the fellows you trained with and they're tops. So glad you could stop by. But to tell you the truth, son, competition here is rough. You know, pediatric surgery is a new field. Two young men started here a year ago, and I hear one's leaving town. Have you tried Pittsburgh? I hear the city is growing. Maybe they could use a talent like you."

The dream of a sunny future was not materializing. I was getting scared. The rejections made Ken quieter; his boisterous optimism went away. As we drove from motel room to diner to motel room, we kept facing disappointing news. I was beginning to think something wasn't right—the plan wasn't working. I started picking at the skin around my thumbnails until they were sore and bloody.

But we didn't talk about it. "Just keep looking. Something'll come up," I'd say to cut through the after-dinner emptiness. "I'll bet you were terrific in the interview," I'd add with a smile. I didn't tell Ken I'd begun to suspect that his plan wasn't realistic. If he went to cities where he had friends, or if he'd done more investigating beforehand, we would be better off. Yet we continued.

The sun was setting outside the dusty window at the Blue Grass Café. The truck stop had a green plastic counter and eight green plastic booths, faded yellow plastic flowers in green glasses on each green plastic tablecloth. I was shuffling through the jukebox looking for an Elvis song because everything in the restaurant, including the cigarette burns on the table, made me feel desolate.

Out of nowhere, Ken said, "I insulted my boss before I left training."

I stopped looking for Elvis and caught Ken's eyes.

"That guy was such a horse's ass." Ken shook his head and hurled his frustration across the table at me. "He ordered me to finish an appendix I was doing *his* way. I can do that operation better in my sleep than he can any day of the week. When I was closing up, *my* way, the guy comes up behind me and says, 'You only respect the men who trained you back East.' I got so mad I said, 'I only respect the men who earn it.'"

I waited. Then I asked, "And then what happened?"

"Nothing. He walked out and slammed the door."

So THAT'S what's happening. No wonder we're traveling thousands of miles looking for a job and getting nowhere. No wonder no hospital is accepting Ken on the staff. No wonder those surgeons keep giving him cheerful interviews and kicks in the groin. I get it. My job now is to get him to make up with his old boss.

I kept my voice low and my eyes down. I tried hard to be calm and not at all abrasive. "Ken," I said, pausing and catching a quick look at his face, "it's good that you told me." I paused again. "I think you've got to make friends with the guy. Send him a note. Tell him you're sorry you were disrespectful. That you think he's a fine teacher. Things won't change unless you do. You need him now."

Amazingly, Ken didn't erupt. He didn't even say no. I felt like I was tiptoeing around some wild animal with a basic instinct to shred any creature in sight. We ate our hamburgers and fries in silence.

After dinner, when we were back in the car, I asked Ken ever so gently to stop by the next drugstore so I could get him stationery. Once again, he didn't say no.

Finally we got to a town. I pointed out a drugstore, and Ken parked the car. "I'll be right out," I told him.

I bought the paper, climbed back into the car, and handed him a sheet, a black-ink ballpoint pen, and a book to write against. "You have to do it. Otherwise you won't ever get a job." I looked out the window to make him feel I wasn't in his space. I waited. He wrote.

When he finished, he thrust the paper at me as if I was to blame. I read the letter. It said exactly what I'd suggested: He was sorry he had been disrespectful. That he had learned a lot and appreciated his help.

He's done the job. No one says the guy can't write.

I found some old correspondence from the hospital and gave him the correct address for the envelope. I got a stamp from my wallet and told him to stop by a mailbox. When I asked him if he wanted to mail it, he barked, "You can do it. It doesn't matter to me."

Think of the big picture. Ignoring his remark, I mailed the letter.

When we got to Connecticut two days later, we visited my folks. Ken had applied at a hospital near our hometown, and the mail waiting for him indicated that he'd again been rejected. Since my pediatrician dad had been on the staff of that hospital for many years, something occurred to me. Without telling Ken my plan, I asked Daddy to investigate among his buddies and find out what in Ken's record was screwing up his future.

A few days later Daddy took me aside. He kept his voice low, as if telling me a secret. "Yes, all the recommendations are excellent except for one bad comment—from his last boss," he reported. He didn't go into detail, knowing that what he was telling me, the news that was the result of his having pulled political strings, would hurt.

A month or so after I mailed the letter of apology, Ken applied to yet another hospital for surgical privileges and asked for his grades and letters of recommendation to be forwarded.

He was accepted. He got permission to do surgery, and a group of pediatric surgeons welcomed him to Long Island and offered him a job. We were relieved and ready to begin a new life.

I'd had a closer look at my new husband and now knew something I didn't know before: Living with Ken was going to be tricky. Mighty tricky.

Ken was to report to his new post in a month. Our next step would be to find a temporary place so he could study for the National Surgical Boards.

THE RAT

The lady seemed nice enough when she opened the door.

"Yes, we're the Kenigsbergs," I told her. "And, yes, we're the ones who called about the ad in the paper. And, yes, we want to see the apartment for rent."

"It's right up those stairs. Over the garage," she said, examining us as she jabbed a thumb behind her to a dark, narrow staircase. She was a big woman wearing a purple- and yellow-flowered housedress and knitted socks adorned with black ermine puffs. Her forehead sported five tiny pin curls held in place with purple bobby pins.

We're falling into modest digs, but it's only for two weeks while Ken studies for the National Boards. And we have to do it, so we will.

So there we were, on our own, with very little money, renting an unpainted bedroom above a garage in a mangy, commercial part of Long Island. The A-frame ceiling was so low that you could stand up straight only in the middle of the room. There were two tiny windows to let in daylight. Worn yellow linoleum covered half the wooden floor. The double bed had a pale pink vinyl headboard shaped like a fan. The fan had a grey stain all across its bottom. After we'd rented the place for two weeks, I bought Ajax and a sponge and tried to scrub it off. But the stain wouldn't budge. Since I was determined to make this work, I asked Ken to help me slide the mattress onto the floor so we could sleep on it without the dirty headboard nearby. He agreed.

Across the room was a student desk with a tarnished brass lamp, a rickety grey table with a hot-plate for coffee, and a tiny fridge for milk and yogurt. Since he intended to study all night, there was nothing to do but go to sleep. Having decided that the place was too depressing by daylight, we planned to go out early in the morning for bagels and the library.

There was a bare light bulb hanging from an electrical cord in the middle of the room. "Hey. Since you don't need that light to study," I told Ken, "I'm turning it off so I can go to sleep."

He mumbled, "Mmmmm," as he buried his face in a textbook.

"Nighty night, honey," I said, as I snuggled into the mattress on the floor, not wanting to look at anything in the room.

A couple of hours later I was awakened by a strange scratching sound. I got up from the mattress and looked around. It was dark, and there was Ken across the room. I saw him in profile by the light streaming from the lamp, his hands propping up his head as he studied from the book. The scratching was coming from that same direction. I followed the sound. I bent down to look in the corner—and there was the underside of the jaw of a tiny white animal chewing his way into the room.

"What's that?" I hissed. "Is it a mouse or a rat or something coming in here?"

I looked at Ken. He smiled, put his finger to his mouth, and shushed me.

"Are you crazy?"

"It's a rat," Ken whispered with an affectionate smile. "He's keeping me company."

I backed away from the rat and looked at Ken through the darkness.

He smiled at me again. "Go to sleep," he whispered sweetly.

Jesus. He's at one with this tiny rat, this stinking room, and his textbook.

"Go to sleep," he urged. "I'll keep my eye on him. And I'll cover up the hole before I come to bed."

He looks like Buddha, sitting there in the stream of light. This is so weird that the only thing to do is go back to sleep.

And so I did.

EARLY DAYS OF MARRIAGE

Once we settled on Long Island, being married to Ken was lots of fun. His personality had power and snap. It's how he started his day. He took long, hot showers and dried himself with a big towel he whipped around his body. He left the towel heaped on the floor—just as he left sponges, sheets, and instruments when he left the operating table after hours in the OR. He dressed quickly: The dress shirt needed starch and had to be white. He chose a bow tie, placed it under his collar, and knotted it as if in one move.

Ken always smiled at me as I made breakfast, then he'd glance at *The New York Times.* He wanted the same menu every morning. Melted Stilton cheese on burnt rye toast, a navel orange cut in quarters, and a mug of espresso. I would walk him to his car after he'd made a side trip to the yard. He would find a flower or even a sprig of mint. He would pick it, inhale the scent, and relish the experience. He never commented about it. He would smile at me as if to say he was enjoying the day, the flower or sprig, and me. When we first married, I would tell him to hurry up and get in the car. Later on, I waited while he completed this routine.

As he pulled the car out of the garage, we had another routine. I would say, "Watch yourself on the road." To his reply of "Yeah, yeah, yeah," I'd say, "Watch yourself or else." Then I'd draw my finger across my neck.

He would wait for that remark, then smile, press firmly on the gas, and accelerate up the hill.

My days involved picking up that bath towel, and making sure he had fresh white shirts, pressed suits, and dinner. I took a job as a teaching assistant at Stony Brook University's theatre department so I could live on Long Island and be a wife. I never thought about my purpose or goal; it never dawned on me that it mattered.

Our first beautiful baby was born. I loved him deeply. Yet four months later, I realized that the routine of baby care didn't make me happy.

When the baby was six months old, I asked Ken to sit with me in the garden because I had something important to discuss. It was early spring, the tender clumps of grass were shooting up from the dusty brown soil, and spindly but determined daffodils were trumpeting toward the sun.

I sat near the father of my baby and told him, "I'm going off the wall."

Ken listened hard. He always did. Even though we were sitting close, Ken squinted at me as if to get a deeper view. A long time passed and then he said, "Well then, get out of the house. Find something you want to do."

Just like that, the problem was solved. My jailer had flung open the cell and told me to fly.

RADIO

Soon after my "I'm going off the wall" confession, while meandering, bored, around the house as the baby napped, I heard my neighbor give a restaurant review on the radio.

Hey! That's Joan, my friendly next-door neighbor! Holy cow! If she can give restaurant reviews, maybe I can give theatre reviews! I have an M.A. in Theatre from UCLA, and I sure can talk.

I called Joan and got the name of the radio station and its general manager.

Wow! I can get out of the house! I can meet people in radio and get a break from diapers and laundry.

I called the station and made an appointment to see the manager the following week.

It was a pleasant April day when I drove to the business part of town. Since the babysitter didn't show up at the last minute, I decided to take the baby, who slept soundly every afternoon, leave him in the car, and stake my desperate claim against the shackles of motherhood.

The office building was of gleaming sandy stucco; the shiny exterior impressed me. *This is show business! A real radio station in this very modern building.*

The back parking lot looked like a safe and quiet place for the baby. No one was back there, and I guessed the cars that were there belonged to workers in the building. I locked the baby in the car and found my way to the station.

As soon as I moved from the gleaming outside through the entrance, I wondered if my plan would be fruitful. The shiny appearance had ended at the door. Two elevators were surrounded by faded black plastic phony marble, the directory was made of tiny white plastic letters mounted on dusty black felt, and the *M* at the end of the radio station's call letters had fallen down into the corner of the directory at some mysterious time past.

The station's glass door was painted a bilious green. As I opened it, I noticed that the darkened brass knob was stuck and unable to twist either to the left or right. Having left the baby in the car and seeing that this radio station seemed threadbare and shabby, I was hoping my visit would be short. I turned to the receptionist, a fifty-ish woman with brassy hair in a low-cut black sweater, stated my name, and smilingly asked for the manager. She smiled back, delighted that someone was anxious to meet her boss, and pointed out that his office was down the hall, past the ripped brown leather couch and plastic coffee table.

His office was more brown than golden and cheesier than most. His door was open, and I walked in to see a friendly guy with haystack hair, a little dandruff on his jacket, and an amiable smile. He sat at a large desk with piles of CD's in one corner. Old theatre programs hung crookedly on the walls.

He asked me about my college career and the subjects I took. He asked me if my husband had a good job and what kind of job I wanted at the station.

Having failed to research the station's programming, and remembering the baby in the car, I got right to the point. I told him I had a Master's degree in Theatre from UCLA. "I'd love to do theatre reviews," I said, hoping things would move quickly.

He chuckled. "*I* do the theatre reviews," he riposted. I could tell he was proud of it.

I envisioned the baby in the car and had to think fast. "Well, I could do movie reviews," I shot back. Smiling again, he looked back at me with a "that might work" expression, pushing the corners of his mouth downward and nodding. *Great!*

He stipulated that the job would pay nothing, but that I could seek commercial support from sponsors later on. The interview ended with his telling me, again smiling, to send a writing sample. I thanked him for his time and shot out the door.

I flew back down the grungy hall, smiled at the receptionist, and scrambled from the elevator to my father's dusty old car. As I approached it, I didn't see the baby. I was terrified.

Where's my baby?

For a second I was afraid he wasn't there. But when I got closer, I saw him, still sleeping in the plaid carrying case where I'd strapped him. The extra blanket had worked! He'd slept and sweated while I struggled to find something more exciting for my life. I was tempted to pick him up and squeeze him in relief. But, deciding that would help me more than him, I let him sleep and headed home.

Aside from the tension of baby worry and disappointment in the grunge of a small local Long Island radio station, I was satisfied with the day. The baby was safe and, although I knew nothing particular about film, I did know something about drama. Besides, I would be in the real world of ideas and performance.

The job was beyond difficult. I had no idea what I was doing. I didn't know how to write radio copy, let alone a film review in twenty lines. Jim, the news director who was assigned to train me, looked over my scripts and told me that whatever I wrote was boring. He kept saying "boring" and I kept rewriting. I would spend hours on a paragraph. Getting an idea. Writing it again so it didn't sound literary. Then Jim would explain line by line what to eliminate, what to forget, and reminded me about the demands of writing for the ear and not for the mind or the eye.

Gradually he made a radio writer out of me. Then he worked on my voice. When to speed up, when to relax, and when to move on. Pause for a joke. Slow down to conclude.

He taught me to wear a headset so I could hear myself speak. Work on a clear and strong voice. Not tentative, not girlish, and not overly sincere. I recorded my reviews over and over, learning to allow the listener time to perceive my words and thoughts.

It was hard work but I loved it. I would discuss acting, directing, and editing. I loved evaluating what made a film worth remembering. I had no trouble explaining why *The Thomas Crown Affair* made chilling entertainment or why the balletic violence at the end of *Bonnie and Clyde* was more affect than art.

Since I was on the radio only once a week, I soon had an urge to become a regular part of the station's team. I asked if I could become a newsperson, work more hours, and be in the newsroom.

The station was willing to give me a try. After the shortest training imaginable, I was the newsperson on Sunday mornings at 6 AM. I got up at 4 AM, put out the family's breakfast, and hit the dark and silent road to radio professionalism. I had little idea of how to get a story off the wire—and even less of an idea of how to write it up with expertise. I dreaded each Sunday morning and had fear in the pit of my stomach as I drove at dawn to the radio station.

It didn't take me long to realize that, although being busy at the radio station was fun, I was not a newsperson.

Since my baby was growing happily and I could afford a babysitter a couple of hours a week, I decided to interview for a film critic's job at the new cable company opening down the road.

CABLE

There was no torn brown leather couch in this place of business. Everything in the cable company's offices was sleek and new: There were studio sets, a green room, video cameras and lights, cubicles for each reporter, a generous office for the news director, and space for editors and editing equipment. I saw what the more dynamic world of cable was like, and I was excited.

The cable news director was younger and less probing than the radio guy. He said that instead of film reviewing I could be a feature news reporter. That meant going out with a crew and shooting a simple feature story. Franny, an experienced cameraman and editor, would be my mentor.

Comfortable in dirty jeans and an old work shirt, his freckled face sporting a wide smile and a two-day beard, Franny was invaluable. He knew what he wanted to shoot and always delivered the job well done and on time.

The first event we shot was a local parade. Franny told me to write a brief script when we returned and we would edit it together before the piece aired on a local newscast. Even though I had no idea what I was doing, he walked me through the experience. I loved it. Finding something amusing about the parade was easy. It was fun matching shots with comments about local kids dripping ice cream down their shirts while the high school band marched by. Showing majorettes, bored, with hips askew waiting for the parade to start was on target.

I felt that I had found my niche.

On the next assignment, Franny and I went to a local Italian festival. We got shots of the zeppole baker, shots of me eating the doughy things filled with fresh Italian mozzarella and swooning over the snack. That made good television. We got shots of the signs, the musicians, and the crowds. Back in the office I wrote up the script. Then Franny quickly put a "package" together with shots of the baker, one sentence in Italian as the baker described his methods. Franny put Italian music under the whole thing. The boss liked it.

On still another occasion we went to the seaside Tall Ships Festival, where the ships paraded along the Long Island coast. We used martial music, and I concocted a script after having found a date or two in American history to make the event interesting.

One thing I learned about local feature television news: It needed a couple of factoids about people, food, history, babies, comments about the weather or the choppy sea or the hole in the boardwalk—whatever made a visually intriguing moment—and not much else.

Video editing was more of a challenge for me. Quick decisions were always hard, but Franny made me look good. The news director seemed to like our pieces, and he arranged for me to do one feature a week. I signed a contract with meager pay and high hopes.

Once in a while Ken would come to the cable station early in the evening to watch the news program live. I think it was fun for him because his work involved people's lives; my work probably seemed like a party. He said, "You did it, kid. It looked great!" after every show.

One evening while Ken was waiting for me, the owner of the company walked through the room. I was in awe of him and asked Ken, breathlessly, what he thought of the man. Ken again got that squinty look and pondered. Then he said, "Shrewd." I thought about his comment many times as the boss grew the company into one of the major cable companies in the United States.

Many months later, to my delight, I became pregnant with my second baby. About the time the baby was born, I got word that the division where I worked was being closed down. I heard through the grapevine that the company was going to grow—and that in order to get a big loan from the bank, our division, which was operating in the red, had to close to make the company look financially solid and merit a new infusion of funds.

I went to my boss but got little sympathy. He informed me that the whole division had been shut down, that it was a company decision, that there was nothing he could do about it.

I was desolate. My baby was two months old, and I didn't feel like I could make demands for another job. There was a rumor that a female newsperson who had worked full-time demanded her job back, was refused, and hired a lawyer to sue the company. I also heard that the company paid her in order to settle the suit. It never occurred to me to do the same thing, since I'd been working part-time and had a new baby. I felt defeated and never thought of fighting for my own interests.

So I sat nursing my beautiful baby and crying as I did it. Ken came and sat close to me. "Don't worry," he said. "You'll find something."

But I kept crying and wondered what I could possibly do that would be as much fun as working in cable news.

PART FIVE

FLYING

59ᵀᴴ STREET BRIDGE

I was visiting Daddy one day in his cramped room in the retirement community. We were chuckling over family matters when he repeated an old tease: "Ken is the smartest man that ever lived."

I decided it was time to challenge him. "Daddy," I said, "you always say that. I want you to sit right down now and tell me *why* you think Ken is the smartest man that ever lived."

Daddy looked amused. He and I both knew I was egging him on to say something definitive. I pointed to the only chair in his room. He sat down, smiling. There weren't many places we could sit eye to eye, so I drew up a footstool in front of him.

First a long pause. His eyes sparkled. He cleared his throat. "Whenever I ask Ken a question,"—another pause for effect— "he takes a very long time to answer me," he said, taking a long time himself to answer, especially with the word *long.* "And," still smiling, he snapped his answer to me, "he's always right."

I laughed because I was finding out the same thing. What a good mind. What a rock. What a source of wisdom. And when I would tell him a problem, he listened and gave me advice.

Ken always remembered whatever he read, and he read whatever he could. Yet the greatest part of his mind was his unending curiosity about everything: the nature of Judaism, trees, rocks, sunbeams, gravity, Marcus Aurelius, politics, medicine, science, Epicurus, the ocean, electricity, gems, gold, and children.

You could call his an outsized life. Grocery shopping, for instance, was a carnival to him. He had a robust appreciation for ripe cheese, big radishes, giant celery stalks, strangely shaped squash, and tiny-grained, pale corn.

Having "encouraged" the family to pick beach plums for him, he made his own jam by using a funnel of cheesecloth that dripped the juice from the crushed plums for an eternity.

Singing the praises of the fruits of the sea from Three Mile Harbor, he harvested clams out of the smelly mud and scrubbed them with a wire brush for hours.

He poached pears in an expensive table wine, creating a delectable dessert. He and a neighbor friend created wine from their own grapes and freely admitted that it was, after a long gestation, undrinkable.

And yet Ken, like all of us, was hardly perfect. My son Amos used the phrase "social cues" to describe what Ken didn't get. Ken dominated most all our dinner parties because of his oratorical and intellectual superiority. People who lived by social cues, like me, found his behavior troubling. But friends grew to love the mind that wrestled with philosophical enigmas, word origins, and amazing but little-known facts. (Did you know, for instance, that Galileo was forced to recant to the Pope on his hands and knees?)

Ken was beholden to nobody. Early in his career he was invited to Jerusalem to teach his surgical techniques to young surgeons in Hadassah Hospital. We stood in a receiving line to meet Teddy Kollek, the mayor of Jerusalem. As we approached him, an aide identified Ken as a "famous surgeon from New York who is teaching surgeons at Hadassah." The mayor, in full Israeli bluster, said, "So what have you done for us lately?" Needing no pause to collect himself, Ken shot back, "I'm here, aren't I?" The two men hugged each other.

Ken didn't want to take time for politesse. At one point he was having increasing difficulty using his right arm. My sister Debby, who was tremendously compassionate, knew a kindly and talented doctor at the prestigious Lahey Clinic who might be helpful. She arranged for Ken to travel to Boston for tests and conversations with the expert.

We went to the clinic, and Ken was scheduled the next day for a battery of tests, which had been carefully planned for an out-of-towner like him. Then Ken decided to go home instead. He never called the doctor to explain why he was cancelling the plan or even to say thank-you. I, of course, was bummed because my sister had gone on a mission to get this doctor. She'd handled complicated arrangements for the meeting to happen.

"Did you call Tarlov?" I asked Ken. We were about to enter the 59th Street Bridge. I was driving. Parts of the streets approaching the bridge were either closed for construction or full of potholes. The road presented a struggle and so did my husband.

"No," he answered.

No? No? What are you, some kind of an ingrate? My sister really goes out of her way to get this big-shot doc. He orders all those tests. Then you break the appointment and don't even call to thank the guy? You should have called over a week ago.

I was pissed. *Well, there's no point in yelling at him now. We're on this antiquated pile of shit and what do I do if he yells back? I've noticed lately that when he yells, he can get nuts. … Who knows? He could even have a coronary or get out of the car. It's generally not what you want someone to do while you're driving and you're going over the 59th Street Bridge. …*

Wait a minute. Why yell at all? Just figure out what you want and get it.

I decided to keep my voice cheery. "Sweetie, I'd like you to do something for my sister. OK?"

"Sure. What?"

"Call Tarlov. Thank him for his attention. Debby needs that because she got him in the first place. Tell him you're grateful for his time."

"Sure."

Done. Another storm averted.

MEANWHILE, BACK AT HOME ... THE TOMATO PLANT

It was a hot, heavy-aired summer day when clothes are in the way and ambition has closed shop. The only way I could get the boys, Matthew, seven, and Ezra, three, absorbed in activity was to round up a bushel of toys and a bucket of water and enlist the great outdoors.

The kids had been dressed up for a morning visit, and I wanted the good shorts, clean shirts, white socks, and new red sandals off for the afternoon.

"You can have water games if you take off your new shoes," I began negotiations.

"OK, Mama." Matthew slid off his chair, took off his shoes and socks, made a game by hurling each one up in the air. He observed where they landed, feeling satisfied with the effect, climbed back up again, and resumed eating. His slight body moved like quicksilver. His hazel eyes danced.

"If I finish my hot dog, can I bring Legos?"

"OK," I said as negotiator.

"If I finish my milk, can I have two buckets?"

"Sure."

"If I put my shoes and socks away, can I run the hose as much as I want?"

Ken looked at me. "No quid pro quos, Mama. Have them do the right thing. No bargains."

"You have to wear your old sneakers for water games," I said, trying to take charge again. But the kid was still at the bargaining table.

"If I wear my old sneakers, can I keep the water running?"

I paused. "I don't know." I was weary.

"I don't want to wear them. They're horrible. They're tough," he whined.

"That's because you jumped in the puddles last time," I said, heading for a fight I didn't need.

"I hate them," squawked Matthew.

"Me too," echoed Ezra, who hadn't made a sound for the last twenty minutes.

"Ken, say something," I pleaded.

Ken moved his chair away from the table, his face wreathed in a smile as he gazed at the rebellious boy. Matthew stamped his foot, displaying the leanest legs imaginable on a five-year-old.

"Come here, Tzutzik," Ken said, his arms outstretched.

The boy reacted to the pet name, pronounced with such endearment. The little limbs, strewn with tiny blond hairs, tender signals of summertime and youth, took him to his father's lap.

Ken asked the boy about his plans for the project. It was as if he and Matthew were the only people in the room. Ken drank in the boy's face, looked deep into his eyes, clearly loving the intimacy. The boy, responding to the approbation, recited the names of his Star Wars heroes. Ken tickled the child's side while he talked.

"Daddy." The boy had turned legislator. "No tickling while I'm talking."

Ken stopped with mock obedience and turned to me to say, gently, "Mama, Tzutzik has done his jobs. He washed his hands before lunch. And he's taken off his new shoes and socks. He's ready for water games."

I sighed an irascible sigh. "He's gonna need another bath, big time, after this."

Ken's voice was tender. "It's OK, Mama. He's done everything right."

Little Ezra, whom I called my chocolate eyes boy, stood in the corner on his fat little legs, observing the gales of laughter and the plans for back yard games.

"Ezra, if you take off your new shoes, you can play water games too," I said.

"Don wanna" came the message from the corner.

"Oh, Ez-Cabez, come up here and I'll have two boys for bouncing," said Ken.

"Water games, water games," shouted Matthew. "I'm going now!" He slid off Ken's lap and bolted out the door. I got up quickly to save the dog, who was clearly about to be whacked on the nose by the flapping screen door. Matthew was too fast for a family dog on a summer day.

From the corner, Ezra gazed at his father and said, "Wanna gah-den."

"Oh, wonderful," said Ken. "Come, Ez-Cabez. We'll go garden."

I cleared the table, put the dishes in the dishwasher, and climbed the stairs to make the bed. *Now all the inmates have been programmed for the afternoon.* Upstairs, I paused to look out the window and see my husband and son in the garden below. There was Ken and this plump little boy with soft eyes and a gentle aura walking up and down the garden rows. Ken's khaki shorts displayed the well-muscled legs of the father, and the little beige shorts displayed the echo of those legs on the boy. The sun cast a golden light on the tomatoes and on the mysterious dark green skin on the squash. The pale corn silks waved with the faintest movement as the two walked by.

A quiet descended. Ken's shoulders and neck surrendered to the heat of the day, the timelessness of agriculture, and the peppery scent of the ripe tomatoes. Ezra caught this rhythm, his chubby legs trudging resolutely after his dad, his socks black from the mulch, and his new red sandals covered with muddy layers of earth. Ken stopped by each tomato plant to learn what had been produced, which buds and leaves needed to be rearranged, which new shoots needed to be rescued from corners of the metal racks he'd placed in the soil when the plants were young.

He picked several big tomatoes and zucchinis, giving them to Ezra, soundlessly and gently, one at a time. The boy carried them carefully to the edge of the garden, where he dropped them outside the fence Ken had installed to dissuade the rabbits from feasting on our vegetables.

Ezra was trying to do his task, but his legs, the weeds in the rows, and the lumpy soil all contributed to his stumbles. Every time he fell, he would get up again, pick up the now bruised tomato, cradle it against his chest and now stained shirt, and continue.

Finally, the two stood at the garden's edge, mud-stained, sweaty, and quiet. They gazed at the garden as if to communicate with it. The father told his boy that he had done very well carrying the vegetables to the edge. "Squas heaby," reported Ezra. Yes, nodded the father, as he put his hand on the boy's head. Then Ken noticed that the boy had his foot on the stem of one of the youngest tomato plants.

"Oh, Ez-Cabez," he said quietly in the boy's ear after bending down. "If you stand on the tomato plant, it can't breathe." The father very gently lifted the little boy's leg off the stem and placed it down on the earth next to the plant.

"But if you stand next to the plant, you can breathe and the plant can breathe." He took a deep breath as if to demonstrate. He took another one to show the concept again.

The boy looked into his father's eyes. He took a deep breath as well. Then he looked at the plant hard to see if it was really breathing. He waited, puzzled. He looked at his father and breathed deeply again. Ken took the boy in his arms and kissed him on the face.

I, watching from the bedroom window, decided I'd seen one of the most remarkable scenes I would ever see. The little boy's legs—with knees bent back, standing firmly on the tomato plant—and his father's gentleness made the black socks, the ruined shoes, and the stained shirt glorious irrelevances.

I'd debated many months about whether to have another child. *There's probably nothing more beautiful than what I've just seen. Yes, I will have another baby.*

A CALL FROM DIANE

The baby had just turned two when an offer for a new job materialized. My friend Diane, who worked for U.S. Congressman Tom Downey, called and said, "How would you like to be the executive director of the Long Island Coalition for Fair Broadcasting?"

I was intrigued. Yet I believed I was totally responsible for the emotional, moral, and intellectual life of my kids. So the idea of taking a full-time job was anathema. I asked, "Is it full-time or part-time?" (N.B.: No professional would ask such a question, and although I was the film critic for local radio and had been a feature reporter at cable, I didn't consider myself a professional.)

Diane, the energetic communications director for Downey, gave a practical answer. "I don't know," she said with a chuckle. "No one's ever done it."

"What would I do?" I asked.

"Oh, Abby, you'd be a natural." Her job was to be persuasive. "You'd talk up Long Island. You'd try to get the stations in the City to give us better news coverage. It would be fun. And Tom would help you."

Ken and I discussed the merits of the job. I said that meeting bank vice-presidents might be a Good Thing because, at the time, I thought they must be pretty smart guys. I said leaving the house every day to work in an office might be a Bad

Thing because I was convinced of those emotional, moral, and intellectual obligations I owed the kids.

Asking my husband for advice was problematic. He lived in a man's world; he'd even admitted to me once, when pressed, that he thought men were smarter than women. I thought he was wrong but just smiled. Still, I knew he believed that my happiness mattered.

Ken listened intently to my explanation of the job, which was ignorant at best. And then he urged, "Do it. Do it. Do it."

And so I did.

The first meeting with Congressman Downey and several corporate executives was an informal breakfast at the Marriott. We sat at a round table in a private alcove of the dining room, the outsized yellow linen napkins and the forks and knives more impressive than the lazy crepes on each plate surrounded by thick triangular pieces of buttered toast. I noticed that the businessmen were all wearing turtleneck sweaters and tweed jackets, so I assumed it was the "at-ease" corporate dress of the day.

Everyone was listening to Downey and seemed to agree with his ideas. After polite suggestions from a savvy public relations guy, it was decided that we would model ourselves after the New Jersey Coalition for Fair Broadcasting, get stationery and business cards printed by a generous corporate friend, and be given office space by the community college.

My first job was to put together a board of directors. Wow. I'd never thought about assembling a board of directors—but what the hell. I was beginning to feel like a big shot. I noticed that everyone paid attention to a guy named Jack. He was from Grumman Corporation, which employed more people on the Island than any other company. Grumman had designed the F-14, one of the great fighter planes used in World War II, and the LEM, the vehicle that took our astronauts to the moon and back. Besides, he had a Southern drawl that reminded me of that "gentleman" caller at Wellesley. Jack said the Coalition should represent a "broad spectrum" of Long Islanders. Everyone nodded, so I figured he must be important.

Then the topic of my salary came up. I was embarrassed that this was being discussed in my presence, but there was no avoiding it. Jack suggested that we have a fundraising luncheon and give an award to the "least irresponsible" New York-based TV station. Everyone chuckled. Someone suggested calling the award a FOLIO for "Focus on Long Island." But no one knew what the second *O* should stand for. Jack smiled and drawled, "Operations." *The military mind has its advantages.*

Since we were about to embark on a fight between New York City-based corporations and us on Long Island, I decided we needed a chairman of the board from a company the guys in the City knew. Since Jack had come to the brunch, had good ideas, looked dapper in a tweed jacket and a turtleneck sweater, and was from Grumman, I decided he was the man.

Although I didn't know exactly what Jack did at Grumman, I figured he might have had something to do with pressing Defense Department cronies for contracts. I asked Downey to set up a meeting for me with Jack at Grumman. I would wear my new turtleneck sweater and tweed jacket.

Jack's office was very masculine: lots of wood bookshelves; a large, broad expanse of oak for a desk; and model airplanes stretching all the way from the bookshelves behind him to the broad windowsill beside him. I'd never seen that many model airplanes.

His office looked to me like a rich kid's hobby room. I believed that all military people thought in lockstep, and I kept thinking of Eisenhower's advice that citizens should beware the military-industrial complex.

But I needed instant credibility, and the glow of profitability and experience that Jack had would most likely fill that need.

Jack stood up to welcome me to his office and offered me a seat right next to him.

After exchanging pleasantries, I plunged in. "Jack, I think you should be chairman of the board."

He moved some papers around on his desk. "No, no, no," he replied. He kept looking down. "I have too much to do as it is."

Oh, shit. What do I do now?

"Please, Jack. You'd be so great. And you have the experience we need."

"No, I couldn't possibly."

Use the congressional card. Now!

"But Tom really wants you."

He didn't move.

I moved to the edge of my chair. He glanced up at me and then again at the papers.

"I'll do all the work," I kept on. "I know Tom thinks you could really help."

"No, no, no."

Maybe he thinks congressmen aren't so hotsy-totsy.

"Oh, please. You won't … even have to come to meetings!"

He chuckled. "OK. But I won't have a lot of time to devote—"

"That's fine. Thank you, thank you, thank you!" With that, I jumped out of my chair and left the office.

The Grumman name is exactly what we need! … Maybe lots of grown men like model airplanes.

I loved the feeling of having gotten a big shot who had said "no" to say "yes."

EARLY DAZE

Fifty ambitious PR people working in local businesses and government jammed into the community college's dingy food court. They'd come to hear the young, brash Congressman Tom Downey announce a new citizens' group that would take on the mightiest TV channels in America: New York City-based television stations. He'd brought along another local celebrity, WNBC-TV's Doug Spero.

Downey had just named me executive director of the citizens' group. He'd wanted me on the dais. But since I didn't have any idea of what was going on, I was happy simply to listen.

I didn't understand why Downey wanted a public event anyway. I figured that if we invited suggestions from the audience, we would have to follow through on them. I was too naïve to understand that public meetings were the lifeblood of public officials. The follow-through was something else.

Downey knew how to work a crowd. "Long Island is a huge part of the New York market, but you'd never know it by the TV coverage," he bellowed. The guy was trim, well tailored, and ready for action. "If you want coverage from here, you have to commit murder. On the courthouse steps. And at 3 PM. Long Island deserves better."

Someone yelled, "You can say that again."

Having presented the dilemma Long Islanders faced, he introduced the irrepressible reporter, Doug Spero. I learned later that Doug always loved convincing an audience of any size that they were oppressed by the nearest power elite—in this case, his own bosses, who ran the newsroom in New York.

Spero also knew how to excite a crowd. The City broadcasters, he reported, had an obligation to report our local news, and they were neglecting all 2.6 million of us. "We should have stories about life here," he roared. "We have good people. People from all walks of life—from factories and schools and hospitals—who make good stories. And we're being ignored! If it's not Manhattan, they're not interested. If it's not a drug bust in Harlem, they're not interested. If it's not a mugging in Central Park, they're not interested. Is that right?"

"No, it's wrong," someone yelled back.

Spero pointed at the crowd. "You got that right."

Downey said a citizens' watchdog group should be formed to rattle the cages in the City and get broadcasters' attention. Then he asked the crowd who should be members of this new coalition. The most adroit answer again came from Jack from Grumman, who, I began to realize, had a lot of charm. He paused just long enough before taking the floor. Then he drawled, "It should represent a broad spectrum of community interests."

I'd found choosing a board fun—like putting together an A-list for a party. Since Downey was a Democrat, he convinced his colleague, Republican Norman Lent, to join the effort. I used the bipartisan approach to get people to sign on. The names of the most successful leaders in banks, corporations, and colleges came from the congressman's lists. My rule of thumb was based on how deep the pockets and how well known the company.

"Both Tom and Norman want you on the board," I cooed, call after call. Everyone I reached was happy to be included.

Remembering Jack's comment about a "broad spectrum," I threw in some major not-for-profit groups and clerics from the three major religions on the Island. Father Tom was the most exciting. A remarkably handsome man with intent blue eyes and an earnest demeanor, he radiated gentleness.

"I think the best thing for us is to visit the general managers in the City," I told Father Tom. "Will you come with us?"

"Whatever you want, Abby." He smiled. "But I'm just a simple parish priest. So I don't know what I can do."

That was a Father Tom joke. He'd spent too much time telling me about his high-powered friends at the networks to mean that.

"You could end up with a lot of power, Abby," he said, *sotto voce.*

What am I going to do with power? I'm here to get those bastards in the City to give Long Island a break. As for you, Father Tom, aren't you supposed to be thinking about men's souls?

One of the most helpful people was not on the board. He was Bob, the community college's public relations man. He came forward after the first meeting to offer office space for me and a secretary. Bob was a racy fellow. He seemed the perfect public relations guy: discreet and able to write speeches, letters, and news releases with a swift and sure panache.

Bob wrote the first letter that the Coalition sent to general managers in the City. I called it our "opening salvo." In the communication, addressed to each station head, he declared that the Community Ascertainment, a process attesting to each station's local community service (required by the FCC in those days), was a "charade." He stated that the service was so bad that unless bureaus were established and correspondents appointed immediately, the Coalition would file against the renewal of station licenses with the FCC. These licenses were worth millions, and no business wanted them in jeopardy.

It was a great letter. Nothing he wrote after that and nothing I *ever* wrote came close to it.

Bob knew a lot about broadcast policy and political maneuvers. So there we were: I was kissing everyone hello and looking charming at meetings, while Bob was writing hot political challenges that would rattle those cages in New York. Some of the other PR people seemed to want the spotlight, while Bob seemed content to get the message out through me. We worked well together. I would bring him my business letters and news releases. He would edit them swiftly and knowledgeably. He was patient and accessible. He taught me a lot.

One day I told Bob that I hated going to the county pressroom to deliver press releases.

"Why?" he asked.

"Because the reporters aren't friendly and they don't want to be nice." (Still thinking of life as a series of dinner parties, I was.)

Bob smiled. "Don't worry about it. Being skeptical is what their job is all about," he explained.

Bob seemed to have plenty of female admirers. So I was wondering, since we worked together a lot and my office was next to his, when he was going to make a pass. He didn't for several months.

Finally, he did. "Hey, Ab. Why don't we work late tonight with some mellow wine. Hmm?"

He got close to me as we sat at my desk.

Jesus. This is so lackluster. He's just going through the motions.

I decided to make it clear in a friendly way that there was no potential here. I didn't move an inch, looked at him directly, and said, "Hey, let's get down to business right now. Without the wine."

He laughed. I think he was relieved. I know I was.

I thought of Bob as a smart and helpful mentor. Later I proved helpful to him. He asked me to be a character witness for him in court. I never knew all the details nor wanted to. I asked my husband what he thought of the request. Ken asked me if I thought Bob deserved my help. I said that he did, and Ken encouraged me to stand by my friend.

The experience was instructive. Bob's lawyer asked me, before I testified, about our relationship. I told him Bob was a valuable professional advisor. When I was on the stand, the lawyer asked me questions that corroborated that opinion. But first, in order to establish my character, he asked me to give the names and ages of my three children. I realized later that as I'd recited each kid's name and age, I was puffed with motherly pride.

Clever lawyer. He knew I'd make a great character witness.

Bob, I eventually learned, was off the hook.

RATHER COMES
TO FOLIO

At the Coalition's second meeting on Long Island devoted to our demand for more TV news coverage, I met Roger Colloff, general manager of WCBS-TV in New York City. I knew he'd been the lawyer for CBS's *60 Minutes* before he became general manager, and I guessed he had to be pretty shrewd since *60 Minutes* probably invited plenty of lawsuits.

His sharp features made me think he was going to be a severe and humorless guy. But when I told him our agenda, he had a twinkle in his eye and an avuncular smile.

I asked him, as I walked him out the door toward his limousine, to return in a couple of months for the Coalition's big fundraiser. He smiled and asked, "How would you like Dan Rather to come to the luncheon and speak?"

Oh my God. I can't believe what he just said! The idea of having the single most important broadcast anchor in America as speaker left me dumbfounded.

I recovered and told him, wide-eyed and stuttering, that we would love it. Colloff instructed me to write to Rather explaining the Coalition, and that he and Rather would travel out to the Island together.

When I told the board what was going to happen, they were amazed. They tasked me with finding a site more impressive than the local college's student cafeteria we'd used the previous year. Board people helped me contact the most prestigious hotel on the Island.

I enlisted a corporate committee from the board to round up at least two hundred guests to support the event. The chairman and I would meet from time to time to see how sales were going. He would smile at me as if we were co-conspirators and say, *sotto voce,* "Get the body in the room, Abby."

I was surprised to discover that Dan Rather looked just like he did on TV. He was a poised fellow—even courtly, you might say. There was a crush of people desperate to be photographed with him. As we were walking upstairs to the ballroom where the two hundred people were waiting, he turned to me and, with a real Texas twang, said, "Now what do you suppose these people would like me to speak about?"

Oh my God. He's not prepared! He needs help! What can I tell him?

I was terrified. I had no idea what to say. I was shocked that someone so famous and well spoken would ask that question. I'd been focused on getting businesspeople to buy tickets and preparing my introductory remarks. I hadn't given a single thought to what *he* should say. I hoped that as he ate lunch something would occur to him. I hoped that someone sitting near him might pass him a good idea.

My introduction, which I'd worked on for weeks and rehearsed with a man from Dale Carnegie, met with polite applause. And then Dan began.

Clearly he had some well-honed stories to tell about early days in radio—like the time he put a record on the turntable and ran out for a sandwich. There was no one to nudge the needle past the scratch on the record. And, of course, the boss was home listening. I'd read his autobiography and realized that he had a plethora of these anecdotes about an unruly youth, more interested in girls than the First Amendment.

Now he was rambling on longer than necessary. He seemed glad to be out of the office and in front of a live audience. He must have thought people would be interested in the minutiae of his life. And yet these businesspeople were not a curious group. In fact, they seemed more motivated to get back to the office by 2 PM.

After fifty minutes the crowd grew restive. I was embarrassed but relieved when someone in the back of the room yelled for him to wind it up. These were the same people who were rabid to be photographed with him before lunch. But by now the Texas charm was wearing thin. He quickly came to a gracious conclusion, and I sprang up to read a plaque commemorating the event and thanked him for coming.

Rather seemed pleased as I walked him to his big black limousine, and I was delighted. I had achieved my assignment. I'd gotten the "body in the room," a heretofore unthinkable task for a Long Island not-for-profit, and the Coalition had made a modest profit.

But the next morning was surprise time. One board member, in a rancorous voice of disapproval, demanded, "Abby, do you think that was a well-done program yesterday? Well, it wasn't. It was all over the place. You have to script it. Plan it out. That's your job. Tell everyone how many minutes they have. Even the keynote. No one can go on and on. Not even Dan Rather. Businesspeople want to be out the door by two o'clock. And you have to make it happen."

Now I knew why his buddies called him "Mussolini" behind his back. I felt demolished, all the wind out of my sail.

I never went scriptless again. I "overcorrected." I wrote the parts for everybody—the congresspeople, the big-time anchors from New York, and the local broadcasters. Anyone who ever participated in the FOLIO Awards Luncheon. (Except the twenty-minute speech by the keynote.) They all received scripts days ahead by fax or mail. Oddly enough, no one ever objected. A few speakers, mostly congresspeople, added humorous remarks from time to time. Yet people seemed to like knowing what to say and having it in large type.

Behind the scenes, my assistant and I created a template for the script. AWARD FOR BREAKING STORY HERE ANNOUNCED BY CONGRESSMAN "A" and DESCRIPTION OF AWARD HERE ANNOUNCED BY ANCHOR "Y." The presenters were in teams of two, usually a government person and a broadcast talent. Each award was announced by one and described by the other. The dais was forty feet wide, so as teams of presenters took turns reading their parts, they could read directions in the script of where to go on the dais.

I thought it was pretty safe to assume that the on-air talent would get a kick out of looking and sounding good in front of an audience of two hundred. After all, their bosses, the managers of the stations, were seated behind them on a double-tiered dais.

Thus the FOLIO Awards Luncheon became a popular springtime happening. The New York broadcasters loved it. Or they at least enjoyed it often enough to return annually.

I made the event as presentational as possible—with brief speeches and dynamic scripts. I'd pair the more lively voices with dignified member of Congress. I'd put the more spirited young news personnel or the racy news anchors with experienced personnel from rival TV stations. It would give the event an edge. And it all worked.

One year the county executive accidentally spilled water on Kaity Tong, a talented and cute New York TV anchor. The next year she appeared in a rain slicker. Another year two congressmen attended who were great personal friends as well as friendly political enemies. I made sure to put them at opposite ends of the podium so they could keep good-natured insults flying. The Irish-American Congressman Peter King looked at his pudgy colleague across the dais and said, "I guess you're late getting here because you got hung up on the sandwiches downstairs, huh?" And his Jewish-American friend, Congressman Gary Ackerman, tossed it back: "Yeah, and you were late because they couldn't drag you away from the bar!" The crowd loved it.

The only speakers who came to the luncheon with their own script were those giving the keynote address. But eventually a board member wanted that modified as well. When Peter Jennings, the epitome of elegance, spoke on and on (very much like Dan Rather), I got another phone call early the next morning: I needed to get the keynote speakers under more control. "Abby," the board member said, "do you tell the keynotes how long they should speak?"

"No," I replied. "But I do mention the timing in two letters I send them beforehand."

"But do you tell them in person? And you should tell them to do something light, too."

After I'd spent years greeting personalities such as Connie Chung, Charles Osgood, Tom Brokaw, and Cokie Roberts, now someone was telling me I was doing it wrong. I was pissed. The idea of telling these consummate professionals to speak for ten minutes and to keep it light was absurd. I smiled at the suggestion and continued to mention the brevity of the time slot. But I never added that board member's anti-intellectual advice.

Besides, I think Rather had been enough in a bubble that he enjoyed the experience. He sent me a handwritten letter telling me so. On his personal grey stationery with his name printed in solid blue lettering, he reported that the trip to Long Island had been "time well spent." I framed it and kept it near my desk at home. After a destructive house fire, though, the letter was lost. I hunted for it in the ashes and debris for a good while, but I finally had to conclude that life was teaching me to lose and move on.

The luncheon that we thought was a disaster didn't seem to bother Colloff either. I would meet with him from time to time to discuss our monitoring of WCBS-TV's efforts to cover Long Island. When I would call him for other keynote speakers from the CBS team of stars, he always obliged. Years later he sent Mike Wallace, a highly skilled presenter. Wallace spoke extensively about defending his position in a $120 million lawsuit lodged by General Westmoreland that had challenged CBS's coverage of the Vietnam War. Wallace was acute. As he spoke, he realized he was speaking over the audience's head. He concluded his speech, and as he stepped off the podium he mumbled to himself, "Wrong audience." I knew exactly what he meant.

Still later, although I knew Colloff was gravely ill, I called on his help again. He told me he couldn't attend but that Leslie Stahl would be there. "She doesn't want to come. She'll have just gotten off a red eye from Romania. She's doing it just for me. But don't expect her to be happy about it."

He had that one right. Stahl arrived angry and unapproachable after that overnight flight. She wanted to speak and leave.

Once she'd arrived at the hotel, she made no effort to find the ballroom where the FOLIO event was taking place. The chairman of the luncheon, worried that we had no visible keynote speaker, said he would search the hotel and find her. He was an experienced and unflappable Long Island attorney, but this situation stymied him. He returned after ten minutes, red-faced and rattled. "I found her. She's in the coffee shop. She's a bitch and she's all yours."

But the new manager of the CBS station had a different way in mind of handling Stahl. He coached me as I left the reception where the two hundred guests were waiting. Quietly, without moving his lips, he said, "Be contrite." I was learning how these managers stroked the talent who gave their stations the panache worth millions.

I introduced myself and asked Stahl to come to the reception. She looked at me with eyes ablaze and spit out, "You told me I could speak and leave."

"Oh, no," I said, ever so quietly, eyes downcast. "There must be some misunderstanding."

"Oh, no," she countered, eyes still blazing. "That's what you told me."

She's one tough customer. I kept my head down and slumped my body in defeat.

Soon it was time to move all the guests into the dining room. I showed Stahl her seat on the dais and moved the program around so Miss Tough Customer could speak and leave. As soon as she was introduced, she took the mic and became the most charming, cheerful, and ingratiating person ever.

She spoke from a loose-leaf notebook with her speech appearing in large type. She reminisced about her unpromising television debut. Her father had called her after the program, and, although she was crying, he was encouraging and upbeat. "Your voice was strong," he'd cooed. "And your tempo was great." Stahl said she felt better. Then she asked to speak to her mother. "She can't come to the phone right now," said her father. "She's crying too hard."

The audience loved her. She left the podium swiftly. But I was half hoping she would trip on her way out.

Every Sunday night my husband, who was very supportive of my Coalition commitment, would tease me about Stahl. That's when he would turn on *60 Minutes* and yell, "Honey, your favorite girl is on TV. Want to watch?"

I never did.

PART SIX

MOVING UP

TRAWLING FOR CELEBS

I'd mastered the art of getting a Board of Responsible Bigwigs and roping in an illustrious chairman from an outstanding corporation. My next assignment was to find celebrities to commend the cause. When a celebrity said your group was doing good work, credibility and power followed. I eventually discovered that if a celebrity was *associated* with the Coalition or *applauded* the Coalition or was *photographed attending* a Coalition function, we were in the "pay dirt zone." Did I mention that if a celebrity was impressed with the Coalition, we were more likely to attract government, private, and/or corporate funding?

Now I had to learn to trawl for celebs! What an exhilarating concept! I thought of it as a kind of sport: To get a big name on my side meant something. Maybe my enthusiasm for celebrity-trawling was a way to prove my self-worth. I honestly didn't know if I was more motivated by the Coalition's cause or my own ego. But, either way, there was work to be done, and I was up for it.

So when a rabbi who was close to Ken and me suggested I call the famous comedian Alan King, I was intrigued. The rabbi mused that King could be helpful. "He's tough to pin down," said the rabbi, "but his heart's in the right place. And you can do it."

I was on it.

"I'm calling at the suggestion of Rabbi Davidson to speak to Mr. King," I said to the woman who answered, switching to my fake upscale phone voice. "We'd like Mr. King to speak informally at a Coalition for Fair Broadcasting luncheon on June 5th out on the Island."

Silence.

"Well, you know, Mr. King can promise you he's coming, and then if he gets a film, he's outta here. He's on the West Coast a lot. You just can't plan on him. He's got a lot of things in development."

Silence.

I decided to press. *I got something in development, too, baby. And I'm not gonna let go.* "The rabbi wanted me to speak specifically with Mr. King. Is he available?"

Another beat. "Why don't you try around three o'clock? He may be free by then."

During the next few days, I tried three more times. The third time: "Oh, you just missed him. Why don't you try next Friday? He's going away after that."

Thus began the "He's busy" and "He just left" barrage within the "King for a Day" campaign. I loved it. The more Alan King became hard to get, the more intensely I wanted him. And I was determined not to let go until I succeeded.

Finally, I got through. "We want local TV to give Long Island a fair shake in the news department," I said to him.

"Look, if you were here, I could talk to you," he said. "This is no good. Try next Wednesday at three."

Then, talking away from the phone, he said, "Hey, Phyllis, take this and block me out some time."

"Oh, hi, Mrs. Kenigsberg," said Phyllis. "Why don't you call him again at three next Wednesday. OK?"

"Sure," I said. *Like hell.*

On Wednesday, loaded with quarters, I took a train to the City. I arrived at Penn Station at 1:10 PM. I got to his office building on East 44th. I checked out the cramped and grimy lobby for phone booths. None. I went out again and found one across the street. It was 2:59. I called Alan King.

"Oh, yeah. Look. I'm very busy today. ... This is tough. If you were close by, we could talk," he said.

"I *am* close by."

Silence.

"Where?"

"Across the street in a phone booth."

Silence.

"Come on up."

Dial tone.

The reception room, where Phyllis, the tiniest and most wizened of women in a grey skirt and tangerine sweater, sat at a desk piled high with notebooks and newspapers, was as grubby as the rest of the place. Dim, dirty, depressing.

Phyllis pointed to the door on her right. "He's in there," she said noncommittally.

King's office was big, dark, and dusty, with very little furniture. His desk was on a two-stepped platform in front of a big window, so I was blinded by rays of dusty sunlight and the outline of this famous comic. Chunky but small. Big head and neck. Tough face with a skeptical expression. He was sitting in front of the desk facing me. No sunlight in his eyes.

He looked just like Alan King. But how he acted was even more interesting. Cautious. Controlled. We talked about the rabbi, our mutual friend. I mentioned how hard the rabbi worked. "That's his problem. You want me to feel sorry for him?" said King. He didn't seem very sympathetic.

I told him again that Long Island didn't get a fair shake in news coverage and that he could help us by giving us support. "I'm not giving you money," he barked. "But I'll be there. You handle all the details with Phyllis."

I left quickly because he was an intimidating man and I felt like I got what I came for. I didn't want to press my luck. On my way back to Penn Station, I gave the phone booth a grateful stare.

On the day of the event, I met King as he arrived. He was driving a sporty sort of van, wearing a rich brown suede jacket with a silk handkerchief in his breast pocket and a smile. His hair was slicked back with shiny pomade. He smelled of some nautical aftershave and gave off a sense of suburban well-being. He was cordial, collected. There was a quiet sense of an animal biding his time. I detected fierce energy, mixed with the discipline of someone who was used to balancing risk with success.

His performance was precise. There was jokes and patter. He recalled his mother and father and their fierce, battle-soaked marriage. Since I sat behind him while he was at the podium, I saw the audience through his eyes. He played them the way a cat plays a mouse. He used every pause for another hit. When a laugh came, he waited. Just when the laugh was about to peak, at an imperceptible beginning of the decline, he pushed. Topped his own joke or, like a surfer riding the wave, knew when to move on.

He was at it again and again. Built a story. Waited. Pounced. Waited again. Patiently built it again. And always played off the laughter. Knew when the laughs would come and, perhaps more significant, when they would begin to fade.

For forty minutes he had a romance with the audience. They loved him. The applause was huge.

We concluded with the inevitable plaque. He glanced at it and suggested that the rabbi, who had been beaming with pride, read it.

The rabbi told me later that King probably knew he would have read the praise effectively. Yet the plan had been to let the good-natured bank vice-president who gave money to the Coalition read it. I didn't know how to disengage the promise to the banker, so the man stumbled his way through it.

The event ended. King went off smiling, having been sustained by the audience and a highly practiced performance. I was ready for another trawl.

F IN FCC STANDS FOR "PHONY"

Congressman Norman Lent arranged for me to attend a seminar in Washington, D.C., created by the Federal Communications Commission for citizens' groups. The event was to establish a dialogue between regulators and citizens about the virtues of media deregulation.

The chamber where the program took place had a Georgian grandeur and impressive dimensions. Six crystal chandeliers hung from the ceiling on long chains enclosed in velvet. In the front of the room were two rectangular tables, eight feet long and four feet wide, side by side and covered in dark green felt. The tables stood in front of four impressive high-backed green leather chairs that faced the audience, where commissioners from the FCC would sit. Each chair faced a microphone, a green leather folder, and pens standing at attention in green marble holders. Fifty modest wooden chairs in rows were opposite the tables for the citizens.

I arrived early, but several members of the FCC staff were already buzzing about. A pretty and lithe young woman in a snappy navy gabardine suit had stiletto heels and a mission. She greeted people with hugs and smiles, checked microphones, and flitted through the green leather folders with great care. When one of the commissioners arrived, her greeting was adoration in its purest form. A crowd began to materialize. FCC functionaries, congressional staffers, and industry lawyers greeted each other with collegiality—as if they were fellows in the same secret society. The ambiance of busy decision-making filled the air. Only the citizens didn't seem to belong.

As the program unfolded, I felt a gap between what the FCC said it was doing and what was actually happening. There was the sober nodding of heads; discussion was peppered with the phrase "when we are able to impose deregulation." What a joke. Deregulation wasn't going to be "imposed" on the industry. Broadcasters salivate for more profit and less inconvenience.

I believed that the idea of the FCC being concerned about the public interest was laughable. The FCC exists to serve the business interests of the companies it's supposed to regulate. No matter how desperate the craving or how irresponsible the desires, the bureaucracy was there to deliver.

When I got home, I wrote a letter to Congressman Lent thanking him for arranging my inclusion and stating that the public interest didn't seem important in the discussion I'd witnessed. I told him I believed no ordinary citizen was ever going to wake up in the morning and be thrilled with the news that the media had become deregulated. On the other hand, any broadcaster would welcome it.

Lent sent my letter to his contact at the FCC. The contact, in turn, sent Lent an incensed letter in which he defended the informational aspects of the seminar. He referred to me as "your constituent" and reported that he had even driven me to the airport at the conclusion of the meeting. He had. But the fact that he'd done a good deed had nothing to do with the fact that the FCC had a problematic hidden agenda.

The unwholesome alliance between the industry and the FCC that I detected that day in Washington is well documented. *The New York Times* columnist Bob Herbert reported that over a certain eight-year period, FCC employees had taken 2,500 trips (I think these would qualify as "junkets"), costing $2.8 million, that were primarily paid for by the industry.

Congress also serves the industry. Broadcasters have extraordinary amounts of cash for campaign contributions. And these same broadcasters hold every candidate's future—via media coverage—in their hands.

Another time I traveled to Washington to meet Mark Fowler, the FCC Chairman. The Coalition Counsel Richard Cahn and I were led into his office and sat on utilitarian beige leather chairs. The office wasn't splendid, but rather reflected a busy man deliberating on a myriad of legal matters. There were somber prints of America's old courthouses on the walls and piles of papers on each table. Mr. Fowler, a slight man with thinning hair and a bookish attitude, entered through a side entrance. He seemed to be in a hurry and offered a mechanical smile. Although the face was inanimate, the eyes were sharp.

"We're a significant part of the New York market," I babbled on before a man with a far more analytical mind than my own. "Long Island buys more cars and sells more retail than any other region," I continued. "We're 14 percent of the New York market, and we get 2 or 3 percent of the news."

He listened. He looked like he'd heard it before. "Complaints like this are fairly routine," he mused, "from Broward County in Florida, from Orange County out West. Even from the folks in South Jersey. They have to watch the news from Philadelphia." He gave a little chuckle here—I gathered it was always open season on the suburbs. "We find that the marketplace works these matters out. As a matter of fact, there's no methodology that works any better. The government, at best, isn't efficient enough to do anything." Fowler wasn't entertaining any discussion.

"But," I chirped, "Teddy Roosevelt, a great Republican, understood that monopolies could run out of control." I wasn't going to give up without a fight. "Roosevelt would have pressured station owners to provide news for all the communities. Citizens in a democracy need that, and we need the regulators to help us."

Mr. Fowler looked at me, stone-faced, from behind frameless thick glasses. "You should really talk to the general managers up in New York. They're bright people. Tell them what you need." I detected a hint of a smile.

Was he throwing us to the wolves?

I LEAVE THE COALITION

After seventeen years, the Coalition and I were afloat with praise and public acclaim. A New York state senator named me, along with others, a "Woman of Distinction" at the state capitol. I was appointed an adjunct media professor at Hofstra University. I had been listed in *Who's Who in the East* (1986–87) and served on the local advisory boards of HSBC, the Anti-Defamation League, the Huntington Cinema Arts Centre, the Institute for Student Advancement, the National Telemedia Council/New York State Chapter, and the League of Women Voters of New York State.

But after the years of recognition and praise, my tasks seemed formulaic. Our events were successful, and citizens had a better idea of how to interface with the TV stations. The TV stations had even improved their coverage to some extent.

If a community organization, which to me was a living organism, remained the same for too long, it was dead. I lost the optimism that had buoyed me in the Coalition's early years. I sought advice about how to keep the Coalition dynamic—I spoke to creative people, civic people, academics, board members, and critics alike. How to alter our "game." How to make it different, more interesting, more useful. No one produced an idea that inspired me. No one said the events were in need of a good face-lift. Yet I felt it deep in my gut.

I met with one smart lawyer on the board. "Abby," he whispered, "get some young kids to do the work. It's going well."

I wanted to leave but didn't know what to do once I left. At this same time the county executive who presided over the community college pressed us to relinquish space for his friends in the political world.

I called the president of the community college that housed our office. "Well, Abby," he said, "the county executive needs more space. And my hands are tied. See what you can do. … You know, you've had the office for free for over fifteen years, and time marches on."

I stepped down. A much younger person, someone with strong writing skills and an ability to conceptualize a new chapter for the Coalition, took charge.

I said goodbye fearing I'd never find another job as interesting, but also fearing that staying in a job where my ideas had run dry was worse. The day I left, a college administrator who worked in the office next to mine said with a smile, "Well, you're finally leaving. Now you're a nobody."

With no specific job to do, for the next six months I was very sad—and very sorry I'd resigned. Out of desperation I audited a course in media literacy at Long Island University.

In the second semester, when the professor, who had become my friend, announced she was leaving for a new job in Berkeley, I asked, in despair, "Who's going to teach this course?"

She smiled as she pointed to me and said, "You."

Holy cow. This is an interesting wrinkle. And I'm in agony with nothing to do. So this may be worth a try.

I smiled and said, "Sure."

I spent a week or two trying to organize a semester's course, but with no success. Finally I asked my friend Harriet, who was a gifted teacher, to help me understand the rigid world of a teacher's syllabus and an unimaginative textbook. I learned the demands of advanced planning and soon had new respect for academia. (Maybe Professor Sullivan at Wellesley hadn't been so bad after all.)

Determined to bring order, surprise, and humor to the classroom, I planned ahead and required my students to read from newspapers and opinion pieces on the subject of media in society. As an adjunct professor of media at Long Island University, I relished honing my own skills in critical thinking. I came to love the challenge of facing some lazy, some motivated, and some mischievous students in class every semester.

PART SEVEN

SOMEONE TO WATCH OVER ME

DIAGNOSIS OF MS

The doctor first led Ken and me into his bamboo-trimmed consultation room to discuss my numb leg. When he mentioned multiple sclerosis, I cried.

He looked like a persnickety man, a suggestion of a sneer on his face and a manner more bully than benign. Thick brown hair slicked straight back, a natty figure in a beige cashmere sweater vest and a subtle tweed jacket. I looked at him, checked out the room décor, and thought that any doctor who dressed like a Brooks Brothers guy instead of a practitioner should be in retail, not remedies. Right then I decided that the "Cashmere Kid" was a good nickname for him.

The doctor ordered an MRI to confirm his findings. The test required that a patient be locked in a tube for thirty minutes. The images of the brain that resulted might or might not reveal nerve damage caused by MS.

The calendar now became the tyrant: The date for the MRI was early in the morning, and Ken was to present a medical paper in Boston late in the afternoon of the day before. "No worries! I'll handle it," I told him, forgetting for the moment that that demon claustrophobia had attacked me a few times in the past.

The idea of under-bed drills seemed to make sense when I first learned that I had to be locked in the MRI tube for a while. There were disadvantages I hadn't anticipated until I crawled under our bed. First, the dust was evenly distributed. Second, the underside of my mattress had some rust stains and busted springs and was about five inches from my nose. I seldom stayed under for more than five minutes, let alone the thirty minutes that originally seemed like a good idea.

As the date for the MRI closed in, I rationalized that "rehearsing" for the MRI tube wasn't even necessary. As I lay in my bedroom at 2 AM with no rest in sight, Ken walked in. He had presented the paper, downed a mug of coffee, and driven three hours straight from Boston—home so he could hold my toe as I was wheeled into the MRI tube to get a diagnosis for the Cashmere Kid.

My multiple sclerosis never did become a major setback. The Cashmere Kid decided I needed an annual MRI from his new machine in his office, plus daily shots with a drug to possibly mitigate paralysis.

When Ken heard the doctor's plans, he decided on a different course: I would get an annual MRI in the hospital and avoid the shots altogether. When Ken discussed this with me, I was frightened and crying.

"Let's talk about this," he said.

He's trying to get inside my brain.

He stood opposite me and took both my hands, looked into my eyes, and spoke in a stern tone. "Your multiple sclerosis hasn't presented in a way that indicates serious sequelae. I doubt you'll ever be seriously affected by this disease. The best thing for you is to go about your life and not let this hamper your activities."

I believe that Ken's positive nature helped me face the disease—and perhaps even affected what happened. Before we moved to Texas, I asked a doctor if I was still suffering from MS.

"You do *not* have MS," he replied. "You might have had it once, but you don't have it now. This happens to a few astonished and grateful people."

As we were packing for the move, I asked Ken, "How did you make me strong and brave enough to not let MS take over my life?"

He leaned against his bureau with both hands, looked down, and then turned toward me and smiled. "Tough love."

"IF THERE'S A FIRE, GET OUT!"

Ken trudged in from work looking pale and despondent.

"What's wrong, honey?" I asked.

"It's a baby who's been in a fire." He slumped in his recliner. I handed him his usual Glenlivet with three small ice cubes and a fast dash of water, which I always had ready for him after a day of surgery. The ice cubes clinked and he sipped for relief.

He still had the sunken mood when he sat down at the table for dinner. He caught my eye from across the table, shook his finger at me, and growled, "If there's a fire, get out!"

He resembled a biblical prophet at such times, wagging his finger and staring into my eyes. Sometimes he delivered a commandment; other times he spoke quietly, more philosophically.

Tonight he was in commandment mode. "If there's a fire, get out."

I liked to be mischievous when he issued directives like this. "What? And not take my fur coat?" I asked.

"No," he said. "Just get out."

"And what about my pearls? Not even my pearls?" I got a severe look, and he sipped more scotch. Soon we continued with dinner and reports about the garden and politics.

Months later Ken went to New York City for his usual glee club rehearsal.

Good. I don't have to make dinner. I'll eat take-out on the couch.

I stopped at Good Luck Blossom on the way home from work. Ignoring the agenda for the next day's board meeting, I settled down with my feet up for TV news and sesame chicken.

As I burrowed into the couch, I thought I smelled something burning. At first I didn't take it seriously. *Maybe it's the toaster oven. Or just my imagination.* I sniffed again and wondered. Now it smelled more like burning rubber. I heaved myself out of the couch and looked under the big oak table (we called it the "Big Oak"), where electrical sockets were cut into the floor.

Crouching down, I saw a narrow string of grey smoke spiraling up from a socket. *Oh, I'll get some water to put it out.* I ran to the kitchen, half filled a big plastic jug with water, and poured it over the socket. But by then the smoke was more than a graceful stream. I ran to get more water and came back to the smell of more burnt rubber and more smoke.

Now I ran to the front of the couch for a better look. *If I can see the fire more clearly, I can stop it.*

Since the couch was really a small loveseat, I lifted it up in one great push. And then a strange thing happened. A wall of fire sprung up not even a foot from me. It went from the floor to the ceiling, six feet wide. I couldn't move.

And then things got even weirder. I had a Joan of Arc experience! I saw Ken's face and heard his voice.

"IF THERE'S A FIRE, GET OUT!" he yelled. And I saw him and heard him yell it again. "IF THERE'S A FIRE, GET OUT!" I heard him sure as I saw the curtain of fire not a foot away.

OK. I know what to do. I'll call the fire department and get out.

I ran to the phone.

Now, for several days we'd experienced an uncooperative and sometimes unresponsive dial tone. And this was one of those times. I grabbed my pocketbook and car keys, yelled to

Gorffy the dog and Roger the cat to come, and slammed the door behind us.

While the cat ran directly into the woods (cats are big on self-preservation), I explained to the dog what was happening. I don't know why, but it seemed to make sense to be talking to somebody. I jumped in the car with Gorffy and headed to the next house on our wooded street.

I rang the bell a long time, but no one was home. I ran back to the car and drove to the next house. Again no one answered. It was a few days before Christmas, and I told Gorffy, "I bet everyone's Christmas shopping."

As I got to the third house, I thought my situation had the makings of a Grimm's fairy tale. I rang the bell. A messy-haired kid wearing glasses, jeans, no shoes, and a big orange sweater came to the door.

"Please help me," I begged. "Let me in so I can call the cops or fire department. My house is on fire!"

No dice. This girl wasn't from the neighborhood and clearly didn't believe me. She was gradually narrowing the space between the door and me. I tried reasoning with her. "How can I get help if I can't get to a phone?" I suggested the next best thing. "Then please call 911 for me. I live at number 1943. I'll wait here until you can tell me you got through."

The door slammed and I waited. Finally she came back and confirmed that she'd spoken with someone. I thanked her and got into the car. A siren, sounding louder and louder, came down the road. Gorffy and I were in our own driveway when the police car screeched to a stop.

I waited for the professionals, thinking the fire was going to be a localized blaze. Eight minutes later, a fire engine came roaring down the street, siren blasting. Then came the fire chief's red car with a big red light rotating from the roof. The siren from the car stopped abruptly. A chunky man with a heavy white beard, outfitted in a navy flannel shirt, a jacket adorned with two rusty medals, and heavy boots, came toward me, hand extended. "Chief MacGregor, District Four, ma'am. What have we got?"

I told him about the little column of smoke from a socket on the floor. About how I turned the little couch over and this big sheet of fire sprung up right in front of me. MacGregor, who looked like a guy in a cod-liver oil ad, nodded. "Yeah, you gave it oxygen." He smiled knowingly. "Any other people or pets in the house?"

"No," I said. "Can I call my husband from your car?"

Playacting like Little Miss Efficiency, refusing to see the potential seriousness of the situation, I went to the car and called Ken.

"Hi, honey. When are you coming home?"

"I'm on the way," he said cheerfully. He loved singing with the boys.

"Well, things won't be quite the same when you get here." I must have sounded like a smart-ass. "There'll be less of a house because it's on fire."

I felt disembodied from what was actually happening.

Soon there were three impressive fire trucks mired in the snowy mud on what was left of our front lawn. Yards of fire hoses from the hydrant at the curb stretched up to the house. The firemen, trudging across the front lawn uncoiling their hoses, reminded me of something out of Currier & Ives. The firemen's hats looked like helmets that Roman messenger gods wore, and their hatchets were from some horror movie.

As the fire progressed, men were running in and out of the house, using those hatchets to break windows and chop up furniture. At times they stopped to drink hot coffee from Styrofoam cups and chomp on donuts that appeared miraculously from one of the fire trucks. And as the night descended, the temperature dropped and the house kept burning.

Around an hour later, the fire chief told me to contact my insurance agent. I called the guy we'd known for years.

He appeared in record time—with a strange tight smile, a clipboard, and papers for me to sign.

That smile of his reminded me of the Cheshire cat's grin in one of my childhood books. "I'm glad you got me right away, Abby," he began. "I can take over this situation … handle everything, once the fire's officially declared out. If you'll sign these papers, I'll represent you to the insurance company and make your life much easier." He stopped for a gulp of air. "I'll get some guys here to board up the house so there won't be any chance of vandalism. And I'll file the papers you need early tomorrow. … Just so you know, there'll be lots of characters parked in front of the house looking to be your agent. But I can handle it all—*and* get you a payment in a reasonable time."

Feeling wary about signing anything but not knowing what else to do, I signed the papers.

By the time Ken came home, the front lawn was piled high with pieces of furniture, screens, windows, shingles, and shutters. The fire chief explained that the fire would soon be declared under control and that later it would be considered officially out. We were not to leave, he said, until the house had been boarded up. "We don't want it being ransacked in the coming days and nights."

It occurred to me that we had nowhere to sleep! Little Miss Efficiency called the local motel and asked for one double room for two adults and a dog. They said they didn't take animals. When I explained that our house had just burned down and our little dog was very well behaved, they acquiesced.

When Ken, Gorffy, and I walked down the hall to our motel room, Gorffy stopped to pee against a standing cigarette ashtray. I made a mental note that life wouldn't be the same for a while.

As Ken sunk into the threadbare coverlet, I think he understood more clearly than I what we had lost.

"Hey," I said. "I think we'll still have lots of photos. Because I never put them in albums like you told me to! But the Bar Mitzvah albums … they're probably gone."

Ken winced.

The next morning he left early for surgery, and I went to the drugstore to buy toothbrushes and toiletries. When I returned to what was left of our house, I was surprised by the number of insurance agents parked in their cars in a single file all the way down the street. Due to a regulation, they couldn't come onto our property. I stepped on the gas and passed them all.

By the light of day, there appeared to be even more debris on the lawn. Then I came to the little flagstone path I'd walked on thousands of times to empty the garbage. Although it was littered with parts of our belongings, the familiar path was now very meaningful to me. I thought about people in wars and why their land, even though ravaged, was so precious to them.

Days later Ken and I moved to a friend's apartment. We'd fished out jeans and shirts for the day from the burnt house. "By the way," I told him, "I've stolen your last pair of socks. But I'll buy you more tomorrow."

"Oh," he said, looking relieved, "thank you for letting me know." I could tell that the tailspin of no order upset the guy.

I learned something important from the house fire: *Things are just stuff.* People asked me how I managed to survive after the tragedy. I never thought the fire was a tragedy. It was a loss—although I did long for some things with sentimental value. For instance, I missed a big drawing our son Amos had made of himself and his dad that had hung in the back hall. It showed a very big man in an orange- and green- and white-striped T-shirt. The man had a big smile and two dots for eyes, holding hands with a tiny kid with the same smile, the same eyes, and the same T-shirt. Across the bottom Amos had written, with a large black marker, "MY DAD and ME." The drawing still exists in my mind's eye.

I asked my friend Wini to go with me to the sooty, unheated house, where layers of cold ash with the consistency of yesterday's oatmeal covered everything. I wanted her to help me go through closets to see what could be worn again and what had been eaten away by fire. She gulped, knowing this would be tough, but responded bravely, "I can do that." And she did—for hours, one cold, long afternoon.

Eventually Ken and I moved into a comfortable new home. Roger the cat came back from the woods and stopped eating the neighbor's handouts. He and Gorffy the dog became friends again.

The only piece remaining from my china set is one little teacup covered with stains of soot that can never be cleaned. It reminds me of the fire that destroyed stuff but nothing real.

MATISSE GIRL

Ken and I were invited to a posh art sale just for doctors being held on a summer night in July. The profits were to go to the hospital's pediatric suite, the art wasn't expensive, and the event was being held in an old mansion next to an apple orchard. Wow.

I decided to wear a white chintz dress printed with floating pink tulips. It was flamboyant, but this was a special night in a fairy-tale setting for a good cause.

Ken usually came home from work drained, in need of his recliner chair, Glenlivet, and *The New York Times.* Yet tonight he looked celebratory. He changed into white trousers, a bold checked shirt, and bright red suspenders. He was cheerful, the kids were happily running around in the yard, and the babysitter was on time.

Arriving at the party, we gave the car to the valet and happily entered the baronial mansion, now rented out for events. The scent of flowers was everywhere. Lilacs and white tulips were in tall silver jardinieres on polished baroque tables. Tiny silver lights twinkled from above.

"Champagne!" one of the hospital's development people proclaimed, wisely curtailing her usual aggressive behavior with the promise of bubbly.

Strolling violinists played as we sipped the champagne, toured the first exhibit hall, and nibbled on cheese bits and tiny breadsticks. Few of the works of art were enticing. But then I saw one that floored me. Matisse's *Le Madras rouge* showed a saucy woman leaning on the back of a chair, her head cocked one way, her hat another. Her arms were resting—or were they posing?—across the back of the chair. I liked her pale face, bright cheeks, and the bright red and blue brocade dress. Matisse undoubtedly knew that if he made her head tip one way, the rest of her body lean another way, and put her hat at still another precarious angle, the tension would be interesting. Was she saying yes or no? Was she waiting or posing? What was behind her smile?

"Oh, this is so much fun," I said. "Why don't we buy it? It's a print—not a lot of money—and it's wonderful."

Ken looked like a kid who'd just been told he had to clean the car before he could get ice cream. He never liked shopping unless it was for ski clothes or fishing gear. "You want to buy *that*?" he asked.

I stared at him, and the fun of the evening, like air escaping from a balloon, dwindled. Still, I said, "Hey, Ken, look how charming she is. Her head is at one angle and her hat is at another. Is she just posing? Or is she relaxing? Or waiting? Who knows? But what do you think?"

Ken looked wooden. No response.

I said, "Well, let's look at more art." Ken sidled over to the buffet to take a plate, four lamb chops with frills, a mound of spindly French fries with jackets, and a big napkin. The expedition to help the pediatric wing was losing ground. I went in a few more rooms then came back to see that Ken was seated with a group of colleagues, all eating too much fattening food and waiting for their wives to finish inspecting the art.

"Hey, Ken," I said. I was bummed. The glamorous night had fizzled. "Why don't we just go home? I can tuck the kids in. And since you don't want to buy anything, there's no point staying."

He looked at me, relieved. "OK. You stay here and I'll get the car." He sounded quite bouncy.

I waited and waited. I strolled through the exhibits three more times and chatted with colleagues' wives. Then I walked outside the mansion, admiring the tiny lights clipped onto the shrubbery to make the night romantic.

Still no Ken.

I sat on a bench by the grand front door. I waited some more. I studied the silvery moon and thought about the grace of the Matisse.

Finally Ken drove up to the door.

"Where the hell have you been?"

He had a smirk on his face, but I was in no mood to figure out why.

"The olives on the buffet were so good I went back for more."

"You gotta be kidding. Jesus."

Ken, who had some zealous Rachmaninoff on the radio, turned up the volume.

Once home, I got out, slammed the door, and went upstairs to put the kids to bed while Ken watched the ten o'clock news.

"I'm hitting the hay. See you tomorrow," I yelled from upstairs.

"Night!" he yelled back.

At 2 AM, when I awakened for a bathroom trip, I saw the Matisse girl propped up against the bureau, illuminated by the moonlight pouring in through the window. The girl, with her tipped hat and coy pose, was right there. In my bedroom. Ken had taken so long to pick me up because he was buying the picture and carrying it to the car. Then he'd brought it up to the bedroom once I was asleep.

"You bought it for me!" I cooed in his ear, trying to wake him with kisses all over his face. He refused to awaken, but he smiled broadly in his sleep then turned over. I got in beside him.

Wherever I am, the Matisse girl is hanging on the wall. That way, I can remember Ken's smirk, the moonlight, and the olives.

WHO'S HAVING MORE FUN?

In the fifty-four years Ken and I were together, some of the best moments were when he would take on that prophetic look and say something wise. When that happened, he seemed removed from where he was, as if thinking about something more timeless than day-to-day cares.

I could usually tell when that kind of thinking was coming on. In some cases it was a cautionary warning—for instance, shaking his finger at me and saying, "If there's a fire, get out!" Other times a memorable utterance would come forth after a simple event. Once we visited friends who had just moved into their new beach mansion. We'd offered to bring champagne to celebrate the end of their arguing with architects and landscapers. As we got closer to their home, the acreage and houses grew bigger, the trees more substantial, and the fences more militant.

"Wow," I muttered to Ken. "They're looking like motels now."

"Yeah, and the walls around them are serious," Ken said, as we drove past cement posts sunk into the ground and supporting heavy metal mailboxes with artfully inscribed family names.

After punching in the code for admission to the property and then again into the house, the host yelled, "We'll be right down!" We were inside a huge summer home, where the light was unusually bright. Long windows and high ceilings brought the outside in. The marble staircase spiraled its way to the next floor. Ken noticed that the thresholds of some of the doors were made of polished brass. He liked that. Proud shining faucets in the shape of great swans cruised at the wet bar and wine cooler.

"It's just too big," the wife fretted. "I never wanted it to be this big. You can't make a meal here without walking a couple of miles."

I raved about how beautiful the house was, while Ken said little except how much he liked the brass thresholds. We proposed a good-luck toast with the champagne and nibbles, then listened to complaints and the hosts' pride in buying the land at a good price. Later we wished them good luck again and returned to our bungalow on the beach.

Ken and I sat on the deck drinking wine. We could see our neighbor Tom and his teenage daughter out on Gardiner's Bay. They were sailing in unpredictable afternoon winds, clinging to a notoriously unstable little boat that kept tipping over. Every time they fell into the water, they laughed, righted the boat, filled the sail, and tried again. Then they would tip over again. With more laughter they would climb back and attempt to set a new course. The boat would tip over again. More laughter. More efforts to right the boat. More shrieks of joy.

I noticed that Ken was quietly absorbing the scene. That prophetic look came over him, and I knew that if I waited long enough he'd say something valuable. I sat right near him and stayed still.

He was looking at the neighbors in the water when he said, "They're getting considerably more joy out of their experience than the people we just left."

PART EIGHT

GOODBYE

THE HOSPITAL VISIT

I got a call at 5:15 on Sunday morning. The doctor asked my sister and me if we wanted Mother to get an endotracheal tube. She was in the hospital with sepsis due to a series of major infections that couldn't be controlled. If she didn't get the tube shortly, she might die.

My sister and I talked about Mother's fragility and the uncontrollable infections. We wondered if a tube down her throat was either kind or useful.

I remembered that Mother had told me, years ago, about her mother, dying and hospitalized and with all her tubes in place, looking up at my mother with tortured eyes. My mother knew then that placing her mother in the hospital as she was dying had been the wrong thing to do.

I remembered that when Daddy had survived surgery and I was in the room when he had tubes removed from his nose, he looked meaningfully at my husband and said, "I don't want that again."

My sister and I decided that if *we* were at death's door and as weak as Mother, we would prefer that our kids opt for no tube. We finally slipped-and-slided into a position comfortable for us: no endotracheal tube.

On Monday, something told me to get up to Connecticut. It was raining hard, and I thought of asking Ken's advice about driving sixty miles in a rainstorm. But Mother was part of me and there was nothing as important as saying goodbye. I climbed into the car, stopped at the office to get things going, and got to the hospital in Connecticut by 9:00 AM. I had a board meeting back on Long Island at 3:00 PM.

When I walked into Mother's room, I saw a leathery and sunken form of her, the sheet up to her neck, an oxygen mask on her face. Her breathing was labored. One eye was opened and cloudy; the other was closed. I went over to her line of sight, kissed her all over her face, and said, "I'm Abby and I'm here. I love you. You're the best mommy." I'd been saying that for several months. I felt it was the right thing to be saying. She loved it. She would smile shyly as if she was accepting the accolade with modesty.

I felt that with very little effort I was making this suffering, sunken soul happy for the moment. I kissed her again. I thought she was very near the end. Later I tried another message. I said, "I'm Abby and I love you. You're the best mommy. Rest easy."

She could no longer speak, but she muttered something guttural that sounded like she acknowledged my presence. The nurse showed me her hand. It was white and limp, more like dough than anatomy.

Her breathing seemed even more labored. I waited a while. When it was noon, I knew I had to leave to get back to Long Island. I looked at her for the last time and left. She died at five that afternoon.

N.B.: If I'm on my deathbed and any child tells me, "You're the best mommy," I may be too weary to chat—but look carefully. I may be raising an eyebrow.

AFTERWORD

When I was young, I thought clothes made the man—or, in my particular case, the woman. Oddly enough, I thought clothes were an indication, to some extent, of a person's worth. Now, having examined myself while writing this memoir, I believe that some of my old ideas, including this one, represented a screwed-up value system.

Today my favorite story about clothes features that clotheshorse of a man, Albert Einstein. If it's true, he had a better attitude about clothes than I did. The story goes that Mrs. Einstein stopped by her husband's desk one day and said, "Please change your suit. The German ambassador is coming to see you." Einstein supposedly replied, "If he wants to see me, I'm here. If he wants to see my suit, show him my closet."

I would encourage anyone afflicted with the yearning to write a memoir to do it. Writing this story changed some of my other ideas. I have a deeper understanding of my mother's love and fears. I gained even more appreciation of Ken's commitment to constancy and truth. I have more admiration for the bold and clever people in the world of broadcasting.

Most importantly, writing this story helped me understand the joys of commitment to something of value beyond one's own daily existence.

THANK YOU

Thanks to my seven grandchildren, who have made my world a better place. As their grandfather would have observed, "They are not phonies."

Raina Melissa Kenigsberg
Joshua Maximilian Kenigsberg
Zachary Michael Kenigsberg
Emerson Daniel Zeeberg
Magnolia Ruth Zeeberg
Lila Ray Kenigsberg
Aster Valentine Zeeberg

Thanks also to the following:

Susan Luton and Katherine Moore, excellent editors and talented friends
Claudia Conner, the typist who brings grace and gratitude to each day
Lizleigh, who brought humanity to Microsoft Tech Support.

CPSIA information can be obtained
at www.ICGtesting.com
Printed in the USA
LVHW031050210320
650785LV00002B/558

9 781532 097515